MW01296025

Pros Titon

Terry Kwanghyun Eum

CreateSpace
North Charleston, SC

© 2017 Terry Kwanghyun Eum

All rights reserved. No part of this book may be reproduced or transmitted in any form or by any means, electronic or mechanical, including photocopying, recording, or by any information storage or retrieval system, without permission in writing from the publisher. For information, address CreateSpace, 7290 Investment Drive Suite B, North Charleston, South Carolina 29418.

The Letter to Titus is translated by the author, Terry Kwanghyun Eum; except as otherwise indicated, other Scripture is quoted from the New International Version of the Bible, copyright © 1984 by International Bible Society.

The NIV text may be quoted in any form (written, visual, electronic or audio), up to and inclusive of five hundred (500) verses without express written permission of the publisher, providing the verses quoted do not amount to a complete book of the Bible nor do the verses quoted account for 25 percent or more of the total text of the work in which they are quoted.

Pros Titon
ISBN-10: 154518352X
ISBN-13: 978-1545183526

For

ἡ βασιλεία τοῦ θεου

My Beloved Wife, Chelsea I. Eum

1st Son, Isaac S. Eum

2nd Son, Caleb Y. Eum

3rd Son, Enoch H. Eum

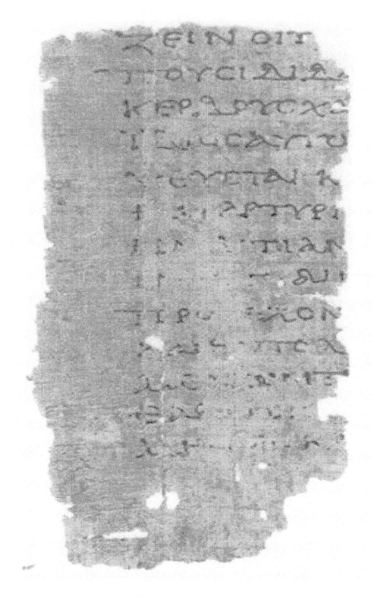

Papyrus 32, 𝔓32 (Gregory-Aland, A.D. 200)
Fragment(1:11-15) of the Letter to Titus

Acknowledgement

Anyone who writes a commentary on a biblical book is constantly aware of the debt he or she owes to others before him/her who have plowed the ground and have surfaced issues that otherwise are easy to ignore. My interest in the Letter to Titus came in a Sunday School class which I taught at Emmaus United Methodist Church at Stratford Hills.

As I publish this commentary, I'd like to publically express my love and gratitude to my beloved wife, Chelsea I. Eum who raises our three gifts from God Isaac, Caleb, and Enoch faithfully, lovingly, and beautifully. Through her supports, love, and encouragements, I am doing the ministry of God for ἡ βασιλεία τοῦ θεου ("*the reign/kingdom of God*") and writing commentaries as a biblical scholar.

The final section of the Letter to Titus looks to the future, that is, the missions of Artemis, Tychicus, Zenas, and Apollos, relatively unknown people who were continue the mission of the apostle. The pericope concludes with a comprehensive blessing. Those who read the Letter to Titus today are well aware that the mission of Paul has indeed been continued by untold numbers of anonymous Christians and that, as a result, the entire church has indeed been blessed. It is now the people who read The Letter to

Titus to extend that *"grace"* to others in somewhere, and perhaps be someone's *"Artemis, Tychicus, Zenas, and Apollos."* May this commentary enlighten you what our God through the Letter to Titus, *"Pros Titon"* is trying to tell you.

Terry Kwanghyun Eum
Richmond, Virginia

Contents

Introduction

The Pastoral Epistles – 1 and 2 Timothy and Titus – are among the most valued of New Testament writings. Yet the Pastorals are among the most discredited of New Testament writings. Why this paradox?

On the one hand, the Pastorals have been valued for a number of important reasons. They helped to establish the classic pattern of ministry and church structure (bishop, presbyter, deacon), which was crucial in the triumph of the early Catholic Church over severe challenges from Marcionites and Gnosticism, and which has enabled the church to endure for nearly two millennia. They helped to establish a pattern of *"the truth," "the faith,"* and *"sound teaching"* as the yardstick and bulwark by which to judge and ward off false teaching and heresy. And, less immediately obvious, they helped to secure the place of Paul within the New Testament canon; the more controversial aspects of his theology (e.g., seeming criticism of Peter in Galatians and a church order without bishops and elders in 1 Corinthians) were made more acceptable by the portrayal of Paul as founder of the tradition, ecclesiastical and dogmatic, by which the church lived and ordered its life. Recognition of this character of the letters lies behind their designation as *"the Pastoral Epistles,"* common since the 18th century.

On the other hand, the Pastorals have been widely disparaged for more than a century and a half. This is primarily because of a majority consensus of scholarship has been convinced since then that the Pastorals were not written by Paul but by a later hand.

Paul's authentic letters (Romans, 1 and 2 Corinthians, Galatians, Philippians, 1 Thessalonians, and Philemon) were written in the middle of the 1st century. The Pastoral Epistles represent one voice in the early 2nd century debate over Paul's memory. The canonical Book of Acts pictures Paul as a culture hero, a law-abiding, miracle-working founder of churches; the apocryphal *Acts of Paul* views Paul as an anti-state, anti-marriage, wandering charismatic ascetic. The Pastorals present Paul as the authority on church administration.

Outline of the Life of Paul

5 B.C.E. – 5 C.E.: Birth, Childhood, Education, Advocate of Judaism

Paul was born of Jewish parents in Tarsus and was a Roman citizen from his birth (Acts 21:39; 22:3). We do not know the date of his birth, but he was presumably about the same age as Jesus, therefore probably born between 5 B.C.E. and 5 C.E. Like many Diaspora Jews, he received a Hebrew name, Saul, and a Roman name Paul (Acts 8:1; 13:9).

He received a Greek education, speaking and writing Greek as his native language, though as a "*Hebrew born of Hebrews*," he belonged to a family that spoke Aramaic at home and attended the synagogue, where the liturgical language was Hebrew. He was educated as a strict Pharisee (Phil. 3:3-5). According to Acts 22:3, he studied in Jerusalem with the important rabbi Gamaliel I, though Paul's own letters make no reference to this. Even if he had spent some time in Jerusalem, there is no reason to suppose that he had seen Jesus. Like all Pharisees, he learned a trade; he became a tentmaker or leather worker (Acts 18:3; 1 Thess. 2:9; 1 Cor. 9:6), by which he supported himself even after he became a Christian missionary.

As a zealous advocate of strict observance of the Jewish law, Paul became a persecutor of the Jewish followers of Jesus (Gal. 1:13-23; 1 Cor. 15:9; Phil. 3:6).

33 C.E.: Conversion/Call

In the neighborhood of Damascus, Paul encountered the risen Christ and became a zealous advocate of the faith he had been persecuting (Gal. 1:11-17; Acts 9:1-19; 22:3-21; 26:4-18). After becoming a Christian, Paul never ceased to be a Jew; he did not regard his call to be a Christian and apostle as a conversion from one religion to another. Though he speaks of his *"call"* (e.g., Rom. 1:1; Gal. 1:15) and describes the experience in language reminiscent of the call of Old Testament prophets (Jer. 1:4-10; Gal. 1:15), in a real sense his encounter with the risen Christ resulted in a radical transformation of his life and can properly be called a *"conversion"* – a fundamental change.

36 C.E.: First Visit to Jerusalem for 15 days

Paul received Christian traditions from the Damascus church, became a missionary in the Damascus area and in *"Arabia,"* and after three years made his first visit to Jerusalem (Gal. 1:16-24).

36 C.E. – 50 C.E.: Missionary Activity in Syria and Cilicia (and Beyond)

During this period on which both Paul's own letters and Acts are silent, Paul apparently continued his missionary work and matured as a Christian leader. At the end of this period he and Barnabas engaged in their *"first missionary journey"* (according to the Acts chronology; Acts 13-14) under the sponsorship of the Antioch church.

50 C.E.: Second Visit to Jerusalem (Jerusalem Council)

The success of Paul's Gentile mission created tensions with the Jerusalem Jewish Christians, resulting in a conference of apostolic leaders in Jerusalem (Gal. 2:1-10; Acts 15:1-29). Upon his return to Antioch, Paul had a confrontation with Peter, resulting in a break with the Antioch church.

50 C.E. – 56 C.E.: Mission in Galatia, Asia, Macedonia and Achaia

Paul launched his own mission and never returned to Antioch. From this relatively late period in Paul's career, some of his letters are preserved and allow the modern reader an interior view of Paul's life and thought. In the Acts chronology, 1 Thessalonians was written during the *"second missionary journey"* (and possibly 2 Thessalonians and Galatians); the others come from the *"third missionary journey."*

50 C.E.	1 Thessalonians (and 2 Thessalonians, if written by Paul), [Galatians?]
54 C.E.	1 Corinthians
54 C.E. – 55 C.E.	Philemon, Philippians (if from Ephesus)
55 C.E. – 56 C.E.	2 Corinthians, probably as more than one letter, Galatians, Romans

56 C.E. – 57 C.E.: Collection Tour

During what Paul saw as the final phase of his mission work in the east, he collected a substantial sum of

money as an offering from the Gentile churches to aid the
Jewish Christian churches in Jerusalem and Judea (2 Cor.
8-9).

57 C.E. – 64 C.E.: Arrest and Imprisonment

Paul was arrested by the Romans during his final
visit to Jerusalem to deliver the offering (Acts 21). After a
series of defenses in Jerusalem and Caesarea, resulting in
two years imprisonment in Caesarea, he was sent to Rome,
where his imprisonment continued two more years (Acts
22-28). In some chronologies, Philippians and Philemon
were written from this Roman prison (as well as Colossians
and Ephesians, if by Paul). He was probably condemned
and executed 64 C.E.

[64 C.E. – 68 C.E.: Release and Second Roman Imprisonment]

According to some traditions, Paul was released and
continued his missionary activity and writing, then was
arrested again. His second Roman imprisonment ended in
his death. In this view, 1 Timothy and Titus were written
during his release, and 2 Timothy from his final
imprisonment (if written by Paul).

Authorship & Date

First and Second Timothy and Titus are called the Pastoral Epistles. These three short writings are similar in style and content and most likely by the same author. That author, however, is not Paul. The writings are pseudonymous, that is, written in the name of Paul by someone else. Pseudonymity was relatively common in antiquity among both pagans and Christians. It was a way to claim the authority of the supposed writer (now dead) for the contents of the document. Sometimes the practice was considered a legitimate way to extend the authority of the supposed author into a new time, place, and situation. Sometimes it was rejected as deceptive. Ancient evaluations of the Pastorals would have hinged on whether or not the evaluator agreed with the author's understanding of the church as a patriarchal household.

The evidence that Paul did not write the Pastorals is overwhelming. There are no references to these "*letters*" in any other documents until the late 2nd century, considerably later than references to the other Pauline writings. The style is not typical of the authentic letters of Paul but rather of a more general Hellenistic literary Greek. The theological concerns and vocabulary differ substantially from Paul's and are similar to vocabulary found in other early 2nd century Christian writings such as *1 Clement* and the letters of Ignatius. For example, the Pastorals use the term *"savior"* frequently, but Paul uses it only once. The Pastorals speak of Christ *"appearing,"* but Paul never does. The Pastorals are concerned with church offices that did not yet exist in Paul's time. Finally, it is exceedingly difficult to fit these letters into any biography of Paul. Perhaps the best guess is sometimes in 125 CE, although anytime from 80 CE to 110 CE seems possible.

The Pauline Writings, Letters

A literary genre is a conventional pattern of written speech that intends to facilitate communication from its author to an audience living in a particular social setting. The epistolary literature of the New Testament comprises several genres of ancient literature. During the last two centuries, archaeologists have unearthed a treasure trove of Greco-Roman papyri (including Jewish) and clay tablets of the ancient Near East. Included in these finds are thousands of letters that exhibit many of the same literary structures, conventions, and functions as the letters of the NT. Although the NT letters resist formal classification, they exhibit no real literary innovation. Their authors were not literati but pastors who employed the standard epistolary conventions of their day; these writers sought to communicate specific messages, not to create an innovative literary genre.

The modern interpreter approaches the letter genre in terms of its overall literary structure, the rhetorical role of its every part, and the anticipated effect each convention exacts upon the audience. For example, how should the interpreter approach the Pauline letters as a literary genre? The letters unfold according to the simple structure of the integral parts, each of which has a specific role to perform in the effective communication of his gospel:

(1) "*Greeting.*" In accordance with the conventions of his literary world, Paul begins his letters by introducing himself (and co-senders or secretaries) before greeting his audience with a salutation. The purpose of such prescripts was similar to that of modern business cards, a convention of today's professional world. Business cards make introductions and help to establish relationships with potential clients. Likewise, Paul greets his readers (or auditors) in order to establish a more intimate relationship with them, thereby providing a positive setting for reading (or listening to) his message and then responding accordingly.

In Paul's letters, however, variations of this opening formula carry important theological freight. Paul intends to frame a rhetorical relationship with his first audience through the phrases he uses to introduce himself, to describe his audience, and to fashion his salutation. This relationship is usually grounded in his apostolic charisma, so that his message is received as instructive if not also normative for life and faith. Sharply put, the Pauline writings of the NT are not personal letters; they are formal "*apostolic*" briefs, meant to be read to the entire congregation as a word to heed and to follow.

Paul's standard salutation combines χάρις (*charis*, "*grace*"), an innovation on the Hellenistic salutation χαῖρε (*chaire*, "*greetings*"), and εἰρήνη (*eirene*, "*peace*"), the greeting found in most Jewish letters. The rhetorical effect of the salutation is twofold: It addresses the audience as beneficiaries of God's salvation and prefaces the subject matter of the letter by the essential promise of Paul's gospel – that salvation is entered into by "*grace*" and "*peace*" with God is the result (Rom. 5:1-2).

(2) *Thanksgiving*. The second part of a Pauline letter expresses thanksgiving for the spiritual formation of the audience. In giving thanks, Paul continues the convention of Hellenistic and Jewish letter writers who offered thanks for blessings received. There are notable exceptions to this convention, however, within the Pauline corpus. In Galatians, for instance, Paul substitutes stern rebuke for expected blessing with striking effect (Gal. 1:6-9); and in 2 Corinthians, a letter to another difficult congregation, Paul offers a benediction for divine comfort where one would expect to find thanksgiving for his audience (2 Cor. 1:3-7)! Since there is no specific addressee, the encyclical letter Ephesians (as with 1 Peter) offers thanksgiving to God in the form of a Jewish *berakah*, a liturgical prayer of thanksgiving. Personal letters to well-known colleagues (1 Timothy, Titus) need not include formal thanksgiving, which is implicit in the intimate relationship between author and reader and may not serve the hortatory character of the correspondence in any case.

In most Greco-Roman letters, divine blessings were perceived as deliverance from some physical calamity or economic ruin. The phraseology of the Pauline thanksgivings is quite different, echoing rather the biblical psalms. For instance, the tone of Paul's thanksgiving is worshipful, often fashioned as a prayer that perhaps could serve as a call to worship for a public reading of his letter.

Paul's thanksgiving is much like a pastor's invocation at the beginning of a worship service, exalted in language and full of important theological themes that will be taken up again in the following sermon. Long sentences are often used by Paul to evoke a sense of sustained conversation with God (e.g., 1 Cor. 1:4-8; Col. 1:3-8, 9-11). Only in this spiritual setting can Paul's letter be heard for edification.

Important theological themes supply the substance of Pauline thanksgiving, typically articulating God's saving action in Christ. Rhetorically, these themes bring the audience immediately to the core convictions of Paul's gospel and establish the foundation for the message that follows. Paul is careful to state the practical benefits of accepting these theological convictions. Here, in the most formal and worshipful section of his letter, Paul remains a pastor seeking to nurture his flock. He does not compose his letters from a scholar's study but from that of a pastor; the concerns of his flock press upon his heart and mind. Interpreters of Pauline writings must recognize them as missionary and pastoral in motivation.

The Pauline thanksgiving often includes a prayer for the audience's spiritual formation. Paul projects an intimate, caring attitude toward his auditors. Rhetorically, this prayer fosters positive, constructive relationship between author and audience. The prayer is also intercessory and often hints at the crisis at hand – that is, at the vital theme of the letter. The words and phrases are not "*devotional musings,*" detached from the main body of Paul's letter. Quite deliberately, they form the basis for what Paul will say to his readers. The prayers in Pauline thanksgivings petition God to resolve the audience's spiritual crisis that has occasioned the writing of the letter.

(3) *Main Body*. Paul next addresses the difficulties that have prompted the writing of the letter, often beginning with a transitional formula or even with a statement of a thesis (e.g., Rom. 1:16-18). While the most important and longest part of his letters, the main body remains resistant to formal analysis. Generally, the style of the main body depends on the audience's social location and the circumstances that occasion the letter. Typically, Paul is interested in defending or clarifying his gospel and mission, he uses those literary devices that help to make his case.

For example, much of the main body of Romans is fashioned as a diatribe, a Greco-Roman literary genre used by philosophers in teaching their students. This kind of formal literature belongs to the classroom, where the teacher imagines himself in a debate with an opponent, who raises questions or makes objections that allow the teacher to argue (and win) his case. Paul addresses his Roman readers, then, as a teacher introducing his students to the grand themes of his gospel. Yet, Paul's self-understanding as a teacher is more deeply rooted in his Pharisaic culture. Recent scholars have made much of Paul's use of Scripture in his letters, in which *midrashim*, or interpretations of biblical texts (whether cited or "*echoed*"), are incorporated into Paul's arguments both to justify a point and to clarify his intended meaning.

Many other literary genres are also used in the Pauline writings to advance the apostle's message and mission. These include autobiography (e.g., 1 Thess. 1:2-3:13, Gal. 1:10-2:21; 2 Cor. 1:12-2:17; 7:5-16; 10:7-12:13; Col. 1:23-2:3); vice and virtue lists (e.g., Rom. 1:29-31; 1 Cor. 6:9-10; Gal. 5:19-23; Col. 3:5-9, 12-13; Eph. 4:2-3; 1 Tim. 1:9-10); household codes (Col. 3:18-4:1; Eph. 5:21-6:9); and portions of early Christian or Jewish hymns and creeds (e.g., Phil. 2:6-11; Col. 1:15-20; 1 Tim. 3:16).

Most interpreters note that the main body of a Pauline letter reflects the interplay of two integral parts of Pauline preaching: the indicatives of theological instruction (*kerygma*) and the imperatives of moral exhortation (*paraenesis*). Paul's use of common moral traditions found in both Scripture and Greco-Roman philosophy is not arbitrary; indeed, it is a remarkable innovation of his letter genre. While the subject matter of his moral instruction was well-known and widely accepted in his cultural world, he adapted it to the crisis at hand to fashion an exhortation that is "*a word on target.*" More critically, the interplay between theology and ethics accords with the deeper logic of Paul's gospel. This deeper logic claims that the acceptance of right beliefs, or what he refers to as "*the obedience of faith*" (Rom. 1:5; 16:26), yields right behaviors as the result of participating by faith in Christ's death and resurrection (Col. 1:9-10). Believers become in life what they have already become in Christ (Rom. 6:1-12). The internal structure of the main body of the Pauline letter, then, envisages this deeper logic; moral exhortation is adapted not only to his audience's particular situation but also to his gospel.

(4) *Benediction*. Letter writers in the ancient world usually added various greetings, specific instruction, and general exhortations to their readers in the benediction. Paul is no different, although he baptizes these literary conventions by adding the distinctive phrases of his Christian ministry. The Pauline benediction includes personal news (e.g., Rom. 15:14-23), general exhortation (e.g., 1 Thess. 5:12-28), more specific advice or greetings to individuals (e.g., 1 Cor. 16:1-24), a recap of the letter (e.g., Rom. 16:17-20; Gal. 6:15-16), and a signature like that of modern letters (e.g., Gal. 6:11; 2 Thess. 3:17), all concluding with a benediction (his "*good-bye*"), typically a doxology (e.g., 2 Cor. 13:13) or prayer (e.g., Rom. 16:25-27) that extends the benefaction of divine grace upon his audience.

Except for the occasional "*recap*," the benediction falls outside the letter's main body, where he addresses the audience's spiritual crisis in a more direct fashion. Paul's concern is for the general well-being of Christian congregations, regardless of the more particular problems of the moment. Benedictions also provide us with a window onto the complex and collaborative character of Paul's mission and early Christian congregational life.

The Pastorals, Different from Other Epistles

The Letters to Timothy and Titus are rather different from the Letter to Philemon. The latter is clearly a personal letter with a single major purpose, namely, the plea that Paul makes on behalf of the slave Onesimus. The Pastoral Epistles are much longer than Philemon; their vocabulary, style, and subject matter set them apart from the short letter to Philemon.

These same features distinguish the Pastoral Epistles from the collection of seven letters generally attributed to Paul himself: Romans, 1-2 Corinthians, Galatians, Philippians, 1 Thessalonians, and Philemon. Of the 850 or so different Greek words used in the Pastorals, not counting the names of people and places, almost one third do not appear in the seven undisputed Pauline letters. Much of the non-Pauline vocabulary appears in late 1st century and early 2nd century Hellenistic literature, including some early Christian literature. The fact that some of this phraseology is found in Luke-Acts has led some scholars to see a Lukan hand in the redaction of the Pastorals. Some of the personal and geographic names found in the Pastoral are also found in Luke-Acts.

On the other hand, some of Paul's most common phrases and some features of his style are missing from the Pastorals. Some of the more important terms in Paul's theological vocabulary, "*body*,' for example, is not to be found. The title "*Lord*" is not a particularly striking element in the Pastorals' Christology even though it is the apostle's preferred christological title. "*Righteousness*" has nuances different from those that the word has in Romans and Galatians. Paul's characteristic "*in Christ*" formula has a different theological connotation in the Pastorals. As used by the apostle, the phrase is to be understood almost in a mystical sense. When the phrase appears in the Pastorals, the phrase means little more than does the adjective "*Christian.*"

The style of the Pastorals is more ponderous and pedantic than the free-flowing epistolary style of Paul. Their style is sometimes periodic with a good use of subordinate clauses and a wide variety of tenses. At other times, the heavy style of the Pastorals is exceedingly complex, with the result that the style of several long sentences is a veritable syntactic maze. In any event, the texts were clearly intended to be read aloud. Several of their stylistic features were intended to increase the rhetorical impact of an oral text that sounded well.

Paul & Titus

Titus was a gentile, probably converted by Paul, who spoke of him as "*my true child in a common faith*" (cf. Titus 1:4). Titus was dispatched on two urgent missions to Corinth, first with the delivery of a very confrontative letter (cf. 2 Cor. 7:6-16) and then with the task of properly gathering the Corinthian gift for the poor in Jerusalem (cf. 2 Cor. 8:16-24).

Even though it is very uncertain, some believes that after Paul's first Roman imprisonment (cf. Acts 28), Titus was entrusted by Paul with the work of the church in Crete (cf. Titus 1:5), where Paul left him to continue and complete the needed formation of the churches (cf. Titus 1:5; 2:15). Summoned from Rome to meet Paul at Nicopolis (cf. Titus 3:12), he was later sent to Dalmatia (cf. 2 Tim. 4:10).

Titus' mission was connected profoundly with the ministry to the poor, dispossessed, and marginalized. His name appeared 9 times in Second Corinthians in connection with his efforts to develop a support system for the poor, a delicate task made even more difficult by the fact of a divided church. At this time of writing he was found ministering to the Cretans, among the most despised, oppressed, and stereotyped people of Mediterranean world. The Cretans were viewed with disgust as barbarians.

(The Letter) **To Titus**

Προσ Τιτον

Titus 1:1-4 → Salutation

NIV	TT
1 ¹Paul, a servant of God and an apostle of Jesus Christ to further the faith of God's elect and their knowledge of the truth that leads to godliness— ² in the hope of eternal life, which God, who does not lie, promised before the beginning of time, ³ and which now at his appointed season he has brought to light through the preaching entrusted to me by the command of God our	**1** ¹Paul, a **slave**¹ of God and an apostle of Jesus Christ to further the faith of God's **elect**² and their knowledge of the truth that leads to godliness— ² in the hope of **eternal life**³, which the **truthful**⁴ God promised before **eternal time**⁵, ³ – in due time he revealed his word through the proclamation with which I have been entrusted by the command of God our **Savior**.⁶

---

¹ δοῦλος {doo'-los} → It means "*slave*," "*bondman*," "*servant*," and "*man of servile condition*."

² ἐκλεκτός {ek-lek-tos} → It means "*picked out*," "*chosen*," "*elect*," and "*choice*." (See Excursus #1: Election)

³ ζωῆς αἰωνίου → The phrase means "*eternal life*," "*everlasting life*," and "*life without beginning or end*."

⁴ ἀψευδής {aps-yoo-dace} → It means "*without lie*," "*truthful*," "*without lie*," "*free from all deceit*," and "*trustworthy*."

⁵ χρόνων αἰωνίων → The phrase literally means "*time everlasting*," "*time forever*," thus it means like "*before the world began*," and "*before the ages of time*."

⁶ σωτήρ {so-tare} → It means "*savior*," "*deliverer*," and "*preserver*."

Savior,	[4] To **Titus**[7], my **true**[8] child in the faith we share:
[4] To Titus, my true son in our common faith:	Grace and peace from God the Father and Christ Jesus our Savior.
Grace and peace from God the Father and Christ Jesus our Savior.	

The introduction of the Letter to Titus takes the usual form of the writer's identifying first himself and then his recipients. In typical Pauline fashion, each element is elaborated with distinctive features (Titus 1:1-41), possibly to give each letter its own personal quality. As with Rom. 1:1-5 and Gal. 1:1-2, the elaboration of Paul's authority and gospel (Titus 1:1-3) may indicate a sense that either or both were under some threat. The introduction concludes with the characteristic Pauline greeting (Titus 1:4b).

- **1 – 4** As in Rom. 1:1 and Phil. 1:1, Paul is described as *"slave"* (Titus 1:1), but whereas the normal usage is *"slave of Jesus Christ,"* here it is *"slave of God."* This was language characteristic of Jewish worship (cf. Neh. 1:6, 11; Pss. 19:11, 13; 27:9), and the great figures of Israel's history, particularly Moses and the prophets, were quite often referred to as Yahweh's slave (cf. 2 Kgs. 18:12; Ezra 9:11; Ps. 105:26; Jer. 7:25). The title, therefore, served several functions: It stressed the completeness of commitment (a slave by definition

---

[7] Τίτος {tee'-tos} → The name Titus means *"nurse."* It is a term of Latin origin. Titus was a Gentile Christian and Paul's companion in some of his journeys.

[8] γνήσιος {gnay'see-os} → It means *"legitimate," "true," "genuine," "sincere,"* and *"loyal."*

belonged to someone else); it was honorific (the greater the master, the greater the slave's authority); and it underscored the sense of continuity with Christianity's Jewish heritage.

More typical of Paul's earlier usage is the description "*apostle of Jesus Christ*" (cf. 1 Tim. 1:1). Typical also is the double attribution of Paul's status and authority to both God and Christ. The distinctive elaboration here is the purpose given for his appointment as (slave and) apostle "*for the faith of God's elect*" – that is, presumably, to bring about and to bring to greater maturity Christian faith and knowledge.

Excursus #1: Election

"*Election*" is a theological language. It is a language of the act of choice whereby God picks an individual or group out of a larger company for a purpose or destiny of his own appointment. Paul presents divine election as a gracious, sovereign, eternal choice of individual sinners to be saved and glorified in and through Christ.

In the Old Testament, the Hebrew word "בָּחַר" (*bakhar*) was used to express the idea of deliberately selecting someone or something after carefully considering the alternatives. Examples:

1. Sling-stones (1 Sam. 17:40)
2. A place of refuge (Deut. 23:16)   3. A Wife (Gen. 6:2)
4. Good rather than evil (Isa. 7:15)
5. Life rather than death (Deut. 30:19)
6. The service of God rather than of idols (Jos. 24:22)
7. Abraham and his seed (Gen. 11:31-12:7)

In LXX and the New Testament, the corresponding Greek term "ἐκλεκτός" (*eklektos*) was used. Examples:

1. Jesus (Luke 9:35)

> 2. The Christian community (1 Pet. 2:9)
> 3. Jesus' disciples (Luke 6:13)
> The biblical writers always use this term in the middle
> voice, with reflexive overtones: it thus means *"choose out*
> *for oneself."*

　　The preposition *"κατά" (kata)* is somewhat
surprising here and could be translated *"in accordance*
with," but usage indicating goal or purpose is attested
(cf. 2 Cor. 11:21). The concern for *"faith"* is similar to
that is in 1 Tim. 1:4-5. It is this faith that gives a
clearer understanding of God's *"ordering"* of salvation;
the word is often taken in the sense of *"training,"* but
the echo of Eph. 3:9 suggests a carryover of Paul's
earlier confidence that he had been given to know the
mystery of God's purpose for Jew and Gentile (cf. Rom.
11:25-26; Col. 1:26-27). For *"elect,"* it was one of the
terms Paul had carried over from his earlier Jewish self-
understanding (cf. Ps. 105:6; Isa. 42:1; 45:4; 65:9; *Sir.*
47:22). *"Knowledge of the truth"* is the same goal as in
1 Tim. 2:4. The phrase that appears regularly in the
Pastorals (cf. 2 Tim. 2:25; Titus 1:1). Salvation
includes a knowing, both intellectual and existential, an
awareness and acknowledgement of the reality of
oneself and of the world. As typical in the Pastorals,
the measure and proof of this faith and knowledge are
"godliness/piety" (cf. 1 Tim. 6:3)

　　The third member of the characteristic Pauline triad,
"hope" (along with faith and knowledge), is
instinctively drawn in 1:2 – as always in Paul with the
full confidence of Jewish usage rather than the

tentativeness of Greek and modern usage. Again the preposition (ἐπι *epi*) leaves the precise correlation of the phrase with its context unclear. The NRSV leaves the ambiguity unresolved; the NIV opts to relate it directly to the faith and knowledge just mentioned, but *"faith and knowledge"* are not repeated in the Greek. Here the confidence is rooted in God's promise and the degree to which it has already been fulfilled. Again it is a question of the evident continuity between a divine original purpose, as revealed through prophet and Scripture, and its due fulfillment announced in the preaching of the gospel (Titus 1:3). It was a fundamental feature of Paul's self-consciousness that he had been given a special commission to make this message known (cf. 1 Tim. 1:11). The confidence of Christian hope was thus rooted in the coherence of a divine purpose unfolding in history and the immediacy of the encounter with the divine in human experience.

In the understanding of the Pauline school, Paul played the key apostolic role in the saving plan of God that extended from before creation to the end of time, of which the Christ event was the center. It is the longest explanation of the meaning of apostleship in the New Testament.

As was Timothy (cf. 1 Tim. 1:2), Titus, too, is addressed as Paul's *"genuine child in faith"* (1:4), here described as their *"common"* or *"shared"* faith. Although we have no other testimony to that effect, the language presumably indicates that Titus had been converted through Paul's ministry (cf. 1 Cor. 4:15-17; Gal. 4:19; Phlm 10); from Gal. 2:1-10 we learn at least that he was regarded as a typical product of Paul's mission to Gentiles. In the two generations after Paul's martyrdom, the disputed issue in Pauline Christianity was who were the authentic heirs and interpreters of the Pauline tradition. The phrase combines the thought of Titus' dependence on Paul and of their mutual interdependence in the faith (cf. 2 Cor. 8:23). In the Pastorals, "*the faith*" usually refers to the content of the authentic Christian tradition, the faith that is to be believed, rather than the faith with which one believes. The greeting itself is the typical Pauline one: "*grace and peace.*" Characteristic of the coordination and balance Paul maintained in his greetings between God and Christ is the way both God and Christ are described as "*our Savior*" within three or four lines.

Titus 1:5~9 → Elders/Bishops

NIV	TT
[5] The reason I left you in Crete was that you might put in order what was left unfinished and appoint elders in every town, as I directed you. [6] An elder must be blameless, faithful to his wife, a man whose children believe and are not open to the charge of being wild and disobedient. [7] Since an overseer manages God's household, he must be blameless—not overbearing, not quick-tempered, not given to drunkenness, not violent, not pursuing dishonest gain. [8] Rather, he must be hospitable, one who loves what is good, who is self-controlled, upright, holy and disciplined. [9] He must hold firmly to the trustworthy message as it has been taught, so that he can	[5] I left you in Crete for this reason, so that you might **set right**[9] what remained to be done, and should appoint elders in every town, as I directed you. [6] An **elder**[10] must be someone who is blameless, married only once, whose children are believers, not accused of debauchery and not rebellious. [7] For a **bishop,**[11] as God's steward, must be blameless; he must not be arrogant or quick-tempered, or addicted to wine or violent or greedy for gain; [8] but he must be hospitable, a lover of goodness, prudent, upright, devout, and self-controlled. [9] He must have a firm grasp of the word that is trustworthy in accordance with the teaching, so that he may be

[9] ἐπιδιορθόω {ep-ee-dee-or-tho} → It means "*to set right,*" and "*to set in order.*"
[10] πρεσβύτερος {pres-boo-ter-os} → It means "*elder,*" "*senior,*" "*forefather,*" and "*presbyter.*"
[11] ἐπίσκοπος {ep-is-kopos} → It means "*overseer,*" "*bishop,*" "*guardian,*" "*supervisor,*" and "*superintendent.*"

26

encourage others by sound doctrine and refute those who oppose it.	able both preach with sound **doctrine**[12] and to refute those who contradict it.

The letter as a whole takes the form of a commission to Titus, and the typical thanksgiving (as in 2 Tim. 1:3-4) is omitted. Notable is the fact that it begins with Titus' responsibility to appoint elders (Titus 1:5-6) and a summary description of the qualities looked for in an overseer (Titus 1:7-9).

- **5 – 9** Just as Timothy had been left at Ephesus (1 Tim. 1:3), so also Titus had been left in Crete (v. 5) (see Excursus #2: Crete). We have no other indication of a Pauline mission to that island, unless the account of Paul's final journey (as in Acts 27:12) had been elaborated, perhaps along the lines of the related account of wintering in Malta (Acts 28:7-11). The purpose of thus leaving Titus was that he might *"set right"* (the only occurrence of this word in early Christian literature), what remains or is *"lacking/falls short"* (as in Titus 3:13). This is not to be taken to imply that Paul's mission was defective, but simply that when Paul left there were still things to be done, as he himself had indicated (v. 5).

Excursus #2: Crete

Crete is a mainly mountainous island in the Mediterranean lying across the South end of the Aegean. It is about 250km long, and its breadth varies from 56km to

---

[12] διδασκαλία {did-as-kal-ee-ah} → It means *"teaching,"* *"doctrine,"* and *"instruction,"*

11km. It is not mentioned by name in the Old Testament, but it is possible that the Cherethites, who formed part of David's bodyguard, came from it. In the New Testament, Cretans are mentioned among those present at Pentecost (cf. Acts 2:11), and later the island is named in the account of Paul's journey to Rome (cf. Acts 27:7-13,21). His ship sailed past Salmone at the East end and put into a port called Fair Havens near Lasea in the center of the South coast, and Paul advised wintering there. However, he was overruled. The ship set out to coast round to a better wintering-berth at Phoenix in the South West, but a strong wind sprang up, driving them out to sea, and finally to Malta. In the narrative of the Letter to Titus, Paul left Titus in Crete to carry on the work.

The knowledge of the island's history is derived chiefly from archaeology. There were Neolithic settlements on it in the 4th and 3rd millennia BCE, but it was in the Bronze Age that a powerful civilization was achieved. Discoveries in Egypt, and at such sites as Ras Shamra, Byblos and Atchana in Syria, show that Cretan commerce had extended to West Asia by the Middle Minoan II period (1st quarter of the 2nd millennium). Throughout the Iron Age the island was divided among a number of feuding city-states, until it was subdued by Rome in 67 BCE.

Chief among these tasks, or the principal way of remedying defects, would be the appointment of "*elders*." Clearly in view are men similar to those referred to in 1 Tim. 5:17-22; as there, presumably the thought is that among the ranks of the "*older men*" there will be some who should be accorded special authority as "*elders*." Although the language is different ("*appoint*"), the thought is no doubt the same as in 1 Tim. 5:22 (*"laying on of hands"*). Notable is the echo of Acts 14:23 and the assumption that there was a church in almost every town. Like Timothy, Titus is expected to exercise an authority like that of Paul (cf. Acts 14:23), as one superior to the elders and overseers whose appointment is in view.

The qualities of the elder (v. 6) closely resemble those listed in regard to the overseers and deacons in 1 Tim. 3:2-4, 10-12. They are to be *"blameless"* (1 Tim. 3:10), once married (1 Tim. 3:2, 12), have faithful children (1 Tim. 3:4, 12), and should not be open to accusations of debauchery (cf. 1 Tim. 3:3, 8) or lack of personal discipline (cf. 1 Tim. 3:2-3). The lack of any mention of deacons here may indicate that the structures of leadership were developing in different ways in different places.

The linkage of thought into v. 7 (*"for a bishop must ..."*) strongly suggests that "$\pi\rho\epsilon\sigma\beta\acute{u}\tau\epsilon\rho\sigma\varsigma$" (elder) and "$\dot{\epsilon}\pi\acute{\iota}\sigma\kappa\sigma\pi\sigma\varsigma$" (overseer/bishop) were regarded as near synonyms (cf. Acts 20:17, 28). We may deduce that just as the elder was appointed from among the older men, so also the more specific role of overseer emerged from that of the elders. We are not yet at the stage where the overseer was a single figure, quite distinct in office and status from other leaders; bishop had not yet become distinct from presbyter/elder. While 1 Tim. 3 distinguishes *"elders"* from *"the bishop,"* here the two terms seem to be used interchangeably. At the same time, the function of the overseer is made clearer by the further description, *"God's steward"* (cf. 1 Cor. 4:1-2);

just as the steward administered an estate on its owner's behalf (cf. Gal. 4:1-2), so also the overseer had to exercise oversight over God's estate (cf. 1 Tim. 3:5) or household (cf. 1 Tim. 3:15).

The qualities of the overseer (vv. 7-8) pick up from those already listed (v.6): *"blameless"*; *"not self-willed, stubborn, arrogant"* (elsewhere in the New Testament only in 2 Pet. 2:10); *"not inclined to anger/quick-tempered"*; *"not addicted to wine"* (1 Tim. 3:3); *"not a bully"* (1 Tim. 3:3); *"not greedy for money"* (1 Tim. 3:8), but *"hospitable"* (1 Tim. 3:2); *"a lover of what is good"*; *"prudent/moderate"* (1 Tim. 3:2); *"just,"* *"holy,"* *"self-controlled."* Again it is worth nothing that most of these qualities would have been regarded as virtues within religious or philosophical circles of the time; two in particular (moderate and just) belonged to the four cardinal virtues in Greek philosophy (prudence, justice, temperance, fortitude).

The more specific and distinctive Christian criteria emerge in v. 9 in the familiar language of the Pastorals: *"holding to the faithful word in accord with the teaching,"* "able to encourage in the sound teaching and to reprove/correct those who speak against it" (cf. 1 Tim. 5:20). The doubling of the language reinforces the impression of a teaching, not necessarily greatly elaborated, but set out in clear formulations that had already become the touchstones for the faith and soundness of profession. Without a clearer idea or what was being thus warned against, it is not possible to determine whether this was a faith-saving insistence on primarily principles or merely a rather conservative unwillingness to allow alternative or exploratory formulations of the same basic faith.

Titus 1:10~16 → Warnings

NIV	TT
[10] For there are many rebellious people, full of meaningless talk and deception, especially those of the circumcision group. [11] They must be silenced, because they are disrupting whole households by teaching things they ought not to teach—and that for the sake of dishonest gain. [12] One of Crete's own prophets has said it: "Cretans are always liars, evil brutes, lazy gluttons." [13] This saying is true. Therefore rebuke them sharply, so that they will be sound in the faith [14] and will pay no attention to Jewish myths or to the merely human commands of those who reject the truth. [15] To the pure, all	[10] There are also many rebellious people, **idle talkers**[13] and deceivers, especially those of the circumcision group. [11] They must be silenced, since they are upsetting whole households by teaching for sordid gain what it is not right to teach. [12] It was one of them, their very own prophet, who said, "**Cretans**[14] are always liars, vicious brutes, **lazy**[15] **bellies**[16]." [13] That testimony is true. For this reason rebuke them sharply, so that they may become sound in the faith, [14] not paying attention to Jewish myths or to commandments of those who

[13] ματαιολόγος {mat-ah-yol-og-os} → It means *"vain talker," "idle talker,"* and *"one who utters empty senseless things."*

[14] Κρής {krace} → It means *"a Cretan,"* and *"an inhabitant of the island of Crete."* This term only appears Ezek. 30:5; Acts 2:11 and Titus 1:12 in the Bible.

[15] ἀργός {ar-gos} → It means *"lazy," "idle," "unemployed," "useless,"* and *"careless."*

[16] γαστήρ {gas-tare} → It means *"belly," "womb," "stomach," "glutton,"* and *"be pregnant/be with child."*

things are pure, but to those who are corrupted and do not believe, nothing is pure. In fact, both their minds and consciences are corrupted. [16] They claim to know God, but by their actions they deny him. They are detestable, disobedient and unfit for doing anything good.	reject the truth. [15] To the pure all things are pure, but to the **corrupt**[17] and **faithless**[18] nothing is pure. Their very minds and consciences are **corrupted**. [16] They profess to know God, but they deny Him by their actions. They are detestable, disobedient, unfit for any good work.

The emphasis is on the ability to refute false teaching (Titus 1:10-14). The description of such teachers is as dismissive as in the other two letters of the Pastoral Epistles (Titus 1:10, 12, 15-16). But particular features suggest that Jewish or Jewish-Christian teaching is particularly in view (Titus 1:10, 14). That apart, the counsel here seems to summarize more lengthy instruction given particularly in 1 Timothy.

- **10 -16** Just as the description of the qualities of Christian leadership both emphasizes virtues that all would commend and highlights the importance of Christian teaching, so also the warning against false teaching both draws on the familiar rhetoric of vilification and opposes it to *"the truth."* Many are *"lacking in personal discipline," "idle talkers," "deceivers."* Such terms tell us little or nothing about the teaching under attack. In view of the parallels with

---

[17] μιαίνω {mi-ah-ee-no} → It means *"to stain," "to defile," "to pollute," "to contaminate," "to corrupt," "to dye with another color,"* and *"to sully."*

[18] ἄπιστος {apistos} → It means *"unfaithful," "faithless," "unbelieving," "without trust in God," "unbeliever,"* and *"infidel."*

1 Tim. 4:1 and 2 Tim. 3:1, the implication is that "*the last days*" are already upon them.

The next phrase, however, strikes a clearer note: "*especially those of the circumcision*" (v. 10). The phrase is the same as that in Acts 11:2; Gal. 2:12; and Col. 4:11. It presumably, therefore, denotes Jews (only Jews regarded circumcision as a positive identity marker); but not Jews as such, rather Jews who, like Peter, Paul, and the others, had believed in Jesus as Messiah and continued to think as Jews – that is, they continued to assume that the way for Gentiles to share in Israel's covenant blessings (the Messiah) was for them to be circumcised and become proselytes. Possibly this indicates that the letter had in view continuing opposition to the Pauline mission from (more) conservative Christian Jews (as in Galatians and Philippians 3). Or possibly this is simply a later picking up of a phrase that indicated opposition to Paul. This could mean, in turn, that the teaching generally resisted as false was that of conservative Jewish Christians or simply that such Christian Jews were one of several factions generally rubbished by the Pastorals. The alternative suggestion that circumcision was simply a Jewish element imported into a more amorphous syncretistic teaching is less likely; "*those of the circumcision*" indicates a group who espoused a distinctively Jewish identity; such people would not regard circumcision as a free-floating ritual easily combined with others, non-Jewish feathers.

This momentary illumination is lost again in the fierceness of the dismissal (v. 11). "*Their mouths must be stopped"* – the image of something being put into the mouth to prevent unwanted movement or speech is clear. That such an action was deemed possible suggests that those in view operated within the churches rather than from outside; but that may press the imagery too hard. *"They upset whole households"*; we are reminded of the importance put on the well-ordered household repeatedly in 1 Timothy (cf. 1 Tim. 2:11-15; 3:4-5, 12; 5:8, 10, 13-14), as again in Titus 2:1-10. *"They teach for shameful gain what they ought not to teach"* (cf. Titus 1:7; 1 Tim. 5:13); the distinction with teaching deserving of support (cf. 1 Tim. 5:17-18) would again be clear by reference to the *"teaching"* itself.

The picture becomes rather more confused by use of the quotation from Epimenides (v. 12), since it indicates that the opponents in view were themselves Cretans (see Excursus #3: Epimenides). There is evidence of several Jewish synagogues in Crete, but the language here implies that such Jews could be regarded as native Cretans (cf. Acts 2:11). The quotation should not be regarded as a careful description, though Epimenides' low esteem for Cretans was widely shared, it falls, rather, into the category of populist denigration, in which the inflated criticism primarily attests inter-communal rivalry or the reaction of a local boy made good looking back on his native place with a jaundiced eye (Epimenides was himself a Cretan). The fact that Epimenides is called a prophet reflects his reputation as a speaker of oracles; it may mean that the writer understood the words to have been inspired (cf. John

11:51) or simply that he recognized in the social commentary a true insight into Cretan character (v. 13a). At any rate, he finds in the citation justification for advising Titus to take a strong line with such people. *"That they might be sound in the faith"* confirms both that those in view were within the Christian community and that the author was working with a well-defined form of faith (*"the faith"*) and with a model of *"soundness."*

Excursus #3: Epimenides

Epimenides of Crete was a semi-mythical 7th or 6th century BCE Greek seer and philosopher-poet. While tending his father's sheep, he is said to have fallen asleep for 57 years in a Cretan cave sacred to Zeus, after which he reportedly awoke with the gift of prophecy. Plutarch writes that Epimenides purified Athens after the pollution brought by the Alcmeonidae, and that the seer's expertise in sacrifices and reform of funeral practices were of great help to Solon in his reform of the Athenian state. The only reward he would accept was a branch of the sacred olive, and a promise of perpetual friendship between Athens and Crete. He died in Crete at an advanced age; according to his countrymen, who afterwards honored him as a god, he lived nearly three hundred years.

According to another story, he was taken prisoner in a war between the Spartans and Cretans, and put to death by his captors, because he refused to prophesy favorably for them. Pausanias reports that when Epimenides died, his skin was found to be covered with tattooed writing. This was considered odd, because the Greeks reserved tattooing for slaves. Some modern scholars have seen this as

---

evidence that Epimenides was heir to the shamanic
religions of Central Asia, because tattooing is often
associated with shamanic initiation. The skin of
Epimenides was preserved at the courts of the ephores in
Sparta, conceivably as a good-luck charm.
(Plutarch, *Life of Solon*, 12; Aristotle, *Ath. Pol.* 1)

That Christian Jews (in this instance, at least) in
particular were thus being targeted is confirmed by the
double description of the alternative teaching being
warned against (v. 14). *"Jewish myths"* tells us little
more than did 1 Tim. 1:4, except that the *"myths"* in
view were Jewish – that is, presumably the sort of
speculations about legendary figures of the past, such as
Adam and Abel, Enoch and Abraham, whom we know
of from the Old Testament Pseudepigrapha. The
second description, *"commands of human beings,"*
carries a strong echo of earlier Christian polemic
against Jewish preoccupation with tradition (cf. Matt.
15:9; Mark 5:7-8, 13; Col. 2:22; Gal. 1:14). In the
Greek, *"those who turn away from the truth"* refers to
the *"human beings."* The implication is either that the
Cretans were enamored of teachings from elsewhere
that, by the measure of *"the truth,"* had already lost the
way, or that the Cretan Christian Jews were themselves
too caught up in such speculations and Jewish traditions
and as a result had turned away from a truth whose
focus and measure were Christ.

The attack on the false teachers continues to use
Jewish categories. *"To the pure all things are pure"* (v.
15) echoes Paul's counsel in Rom. 14:14 and 20. The

37

imagery is that of the laws of clean and unclean, which were so fundamental to Jewish identity (cf. *1 Macc.* 1:62-63; Mark 7:1-23; Acts 10:14). In the context of the Temple (on which the purity laws centered), all things were indeed clean/pure; they had to be. So the worshiper, on entering the Temple duly purified, could be confident that nothing and no one touched would render him or her impure. Paul had extended the principle: For the believer cleansed by faith (cf. Acts 15:9), the previous sharp distinction between sacred and secular had been broken down; all things given by God for human use (unclean food as well) could properly be regarded as clean (cf. Rom. 14:14, 20; 1 Tim. 4:4). The principle is that purity before God is primary: If God has accepted someone, the secondary human regulations about acceptable and unacceptable are irrelevant. In these circumstances, since God ignores such regulations, so can those accepted by God.

The opposite principle, which in fact underlays the laws of clean and unclean, is that impurity contaminates. *"The corrupt"* (μιαίνω *miaino*) uses a verb also drawn from the sphere of ceremonial impurity (as in John 18:28), though used here of moral defilement through sins and vices. Everything that such people touch is thereby rendered impure – here in particular their minds and conscience. If, indeed, the teachers under attack here were Christian Jews or those heavily influenced by Jewish tradition, the logic would likely have powerful effect.

The final dismissive attack is on their Christian profession (v. 16): *"They profess to know God, but deny*

him by what they do." The thought is similar to that of
2 Tim. 3:5. Is there a link to the claimed (higher)
"*knowledge*" of 1 Tim. 6:20? Not necessarily; the verb
is different, and for Paul knowledge of God is the most
fundamental description of true religion (cf. Rom. 1:21;
1 Cor. 1:21; 1 Thess. 4:5). It is not a higher knowledge
of God that is disputed, but the basic claim to "*know*"
God at all. Here, as in Matt. 7:16, the fruit produced is
evidence of the character of the tree; we might also note
the echo of Ps. 14:1. Implicit once again is the
conviction that the writer's understanding of "*godliness*"
is a measure of what is acceptable to God and what is
not. The final clause reverts to vilification –
"*abominable*," "*detestable*" (echoing the Jewish horror
of idolatry; cf. Deut. 29:17), "*disobedient* (cf. Titus 3:3),
"*unfit* (cf. 2 Tim. 3:8) *for any good work.*"

Titus 2:1~10 → Instructions for the Christian Household

NIV	TT
2 [1] You, however, must teach what is appropriate to sound doctrine. [2] Teach the older men to be temperate, worthy of respect, self-controlled, and sound in faith, in love and in endurance.	**2** [1] But as for you, speak what is consistent with sound doctrine. [2] Tell the **older men**[19] to be temperate, serious, prudent, and sound in faith, in love, and in endurance.
[3] Likewise, teach the older women to be reverent in the way they live, not to be slanderers or addicted too much wine, but to teach what is good. [4] Then they can urge the younger women to love their husbands and children, [5] to be self-controlled and pure, to be busy at home, to be kind, and to be subject to their husbands, so that no	[3] Likewise, tell the **older women**[20] to be **reverent**[21] in behavior, not to be slanderers or slaves to drink; they are to teach what is good, [4] so that they may **train**[22] the young women to love their husbands, to love their children, [5] to be self-controlled, chaste, good managers of the household, kind, being **submissive**[23] to their husbands, so that the word of God may not be

[19] πρεσβύτης {pres-boo-tace} → It means *"elderly," "old man," "aged man,"* and *"ambassador."* Generally it means a man aged in the 50s or 60s.

[20] πρεσβῦτις {pres-boo-tis} → It means *"aged woman,"* and *"elderly woman."*

[21] ἱεροπρεπής {hee-er-op-rep-ace} → It means *"sacred things to God," "reverent," "become holiness," "worthy of reverence,"* and *"holy."*

[22] σωφρονίζω {sophronizo} → It means *"restore one to his senses," "to moderate," "to control," "to disciple," "to encourage," "to advise,"* and *"to urge."*

[23] ὑποτάσσω {hoop-otasso} → It means *"to subordinate," "to subject," "to submit," "to obey,"* and *"become subject."*

one will malign the word of God. [6] Similarly, encourage the young men to be self-controlled. [7] In everything set them an example by doing what is good. In your teaching show integrity, seriousness [8] and soundness of speech that cannot be condemned, so that those who oppose you may be ashamed because they have nothing bad to say about us. [9] Teach slaves to be subject to their masters in everything, to try to please them, not to talk back to them, [10] and not to steal from them, but to show that they can be fully trusted, so that in every way they will make the teaching about God our Savior attractive.	discredited. [6] Likewise, urge the younger men to **be reasonable**[24]. [7] Show yourself in all respects a model of good works, and in your teaching show integrity, gravity, [8] and sound speech that cannot be censured; then any opponent will be put to shame, having nothing evil to say of us. [9] Tell slaves to be submissive to their masters and to be **acceptable**[25] in everything; they are not to talk back, [10] not to **put aside for oneself**[26], but to show complete and perfect fidelity, so that in everything they may be **an ornament**[27] to the doctrine of God our Savior.

In this section the author adapts the traditional form of the household code in order to present instructions to

---

[24] σωφρονέω {sophroneo} → It means *"to exercise self control," "be in right mind," "be sober," "be of sound mind," "be reasonable," "be sensible,"* and *"be serious."*

[25] εὐάρεστος {yoo-ar-es-tos} → It means *"acceptably," "well pleasing," "please well,"* and *"acceptable."*

[26] νοσφίζω {nos-fi-zo} → It means *"put aside for oneself," "misappropriate," "to purloin," "to embezzle," "to withdraw covertly," "to separate,"* and *"to divide."*

[27] κοσμέω {kos-meh-o} → It means *"to put in order," "to ornament," "adore," "make ready," "prepare," "make beautiful," "attractive," "do credit to,"* and *"to decorate."*

various groups in the Christian household, the church (cf. 1 Tim. 3:15; Col. 3:18-4:1; 1 Pet. 2:11-3:12). Thought written to *"Titus,"* the literary form of the pseudepigraphical letter serves as the vehicle for instructions to the church as a whole. While in the author's context he believed it was appropriate that only authorized men serve in teaching roles (cf. 1 Tim. 2:11-15), every Christian of whatever status in any social situation can serve as a teacher of the faith by the way he or she reflects the faith in daily life.

- **1 – 10** Christian life is based on Christian theology, how the faith is understood. Doctrine (see Excursus #4: Doctrine) is not merely abstract and theoretical, but the basis for life.

Excursus #4: Doctrine

The Greek word for *"Doctrine"* is *"διδασκαλία"* (*didaskalia*) which also can mean *"instruction," "teaching."* The term appears 21 times in the New Testament. Many times in the New Testament, the word was translated as (1) *"teaching"* (e.g., Jesus' teaching, teachings of the Pharisees, teachings of people cf. Matt. 15:9; Eph. 4:14; Col. 2:22; Rom. 12:7).

However, in the Pastoral Epistles, the majority of occurrences of *"διδασκαλία"* are in the context of (2) doctrine of the church or *"sound doctrine"* (cf. 1 Tim. 1:10; 4:6, 13, 16; 5:17; 6:1; 2 Tim. 4:3; Titus 1:9; 2:7, 10). Lastly, *"διδασκαλία"* refers to (3) the Old Testament in Rom. 15:4.

The letter to Titus shares with 1 Timothy a concern for good household management, no doubt both as a test of leadership (cf. Titus 1:6) and as a model for good church management (cf. 1 Tim. 3:4-5, 12). In its compactness, the outline here comes closer to the model *Haustafel* (guidelines for good household management) found in Col. 3:18-4:1 than does any other in that all the elements of the typical household of the time are present: wives, husbands, children (cc. 4-5), slaves, and masters (vv. 9-10) (see Excursus #5: *Haustafel*). The slant of this passage, however, reflects the same distinctive concern displayed in 1 Timothy 5 over the older men and women (vv. 2-3) and places the responsibility for counseling wives on the older women (vv. 4-5). The responsibilities of younger men, and Titus, are likewise inserted (vv. 6-8). Unusually, no word of counsel is given to the primary male member of the household: the husband, father and master (cf. Col. 3:19, 21; 4:1). The implication may be that in the household of the church that role is to be filled by Titus. Unlike 1 Tim. 5:3-6, there seems to be no problem regarding the rights and responsibilities of widows.

The focus now switches to Titus' own positive teaching (v. 1). He must speak *"what is fitting, appropriate to sound doctrine."* Once again we not that there is a criterion and measure of acceptable teaching, what we might call the agreed syllabus of confessional claims and acceptable conduct.

Somewhat surprisingly, the first example of such teaching is the advice of how older men should conduct themselves. Also somewhat surprising is the fact that the commendatory virtues listed are so similar to those used in 1 Timothy 3, particularly in reference to the overseer; the older men are to be temperate (cf. 1 Tim. 3:2, 11); respectable, dignified, serious (cf. 1 Tim. 3:8); prudent, moderate (cf. Titus 1:8; 1 Tim. 3:2); sound in faith (cf. 1 Tim. 3:9), in love (cf. 2 Tim. 1:13), and in patience (cf. 2 Tim. 3:10). At the very least, the overlap confirms that the obvious place to look for leadership in the churches was from among the ranks of the older, more experienced, wiser men.

As in 1 Tim. 5:1-2, thought of responsibility toward the older men prompts a matching reflection on the role of older women (v. 3). What is striking here is the extent of the responsibility put upon them and the language used for them. Their *"behavior/demeanor"* should be *"as befits a priest"* (NIV and NRSV, *"reverent"*). The imagery would be surprising only if earliest Christianity had retained an office of priest and confined it to men. But Paul's language elsewhere indicates that he saw all ministry of the gospel as priestly in character (cf. Rom. 15:16; Phil. 2:25); the *"royal priesthood"* of 1 Pet. 2:9 was not gender related. So here, it evidently did not jar to associate the image of priest with the older women. They, too, could exercise a priestly ministry in serving the gospel (cf. 1 Tim. 5:3-19) or by their personal dedication (cf. Rom. 12:1-2, the priestly task of offering their bodies as a sacrifice).

The following vices to be avoided give a more negative view of the women, but in fact accord with what was said regarding deacons in 1 Tim. 3: *"not slanderers"* (cf. 1 Tim. 3:11), *"not enslaved to much wine"* (cf. 1 Tim. 3:8). Perhaps most surprising of all,

in view of 1 Tim. 2:12, is the next criterion: They are to
be *"teachers of what is good."* However, it becomes
clear in vv. 4-5 that the teaching role of the older
women is in reference to younger women.
Nevertheless, the responsibility put upon the older
women here is significantly larger than that envisaged
in 1 Tim. 5:5, 10. Here again the clear assumption is
that the older person has a responsibility to pass on to
the next generation the wisdom gained through the
years.

The specific term *"σωφρονίζω"* (*sophronizo*) can be
translated quite strongly as *"bring the younger women
to their senses,"* but it may have the weaker sense of
"encourage," "advise," "urge" (v. 4). Particularly in
view is the role of the matriarch within the household:
to encourage the wife of the household to "love her
husband and love her children." That the wife's or the
husband's mother should be given such respect within
the household would be taken for granted; no hint is
given of the pressures on the young wife under the
authority of both her husband and her mother (-in-law),
but they do not take much imaging.

Like the older men (v.2) the younger women are to
be encouraged to be prudent, moderate, perhaps here
with the overtone of *"chaste/modest/pure,"* like
Timothy (cf. 1 Tim. 5:22), *"house-keepers," "working
at home."* More characteristic of the codes of good
household management is the counsel that they should
be *"submissive"* to their husbands. As elsewhere the
concern was lest the liberating message of the gospel
might encourage Christian women to ignore or react

against the patterns of sound household management and so bring the message of the gospel into disrepute as antisocial and destructive of the good order of society's basic unit (cf. 1 Tim. 3:7).

If the responsibility for instructing the younger women was primarily that of the older women, the responsibility for instructing the younger men belongs to Titus himself (v. 6). They are to be *"reasonable/sensible"* (σωφρονέω *sophron*; the same range of words denoting a highly prized virtue in Greek circles; both the NIV and the NRSV prefer *"self-controlled"*). Titus has to present himself as a *"model of good works"* (v. 7), in his teaching *"incorrupt,"* *"respectable,"* *"dignified,"* *"serious,"* *"sound"* in preaching that is *"beyond reproach."* The objective is that *"he who is opposed might be put to shame at having nothing bad to say about us"* (v. 8). Worth noting, once again, is the concern for a good reputation and the assumption that behavior worthy of criticism on the part of Titus would reflect badly on the whole community (*"us"*).

As in other household codes, the responsibility of slaves to their masters is given final prominent place (vv.9-10). The fact that the same term (ὑποτάσσω, *hypotasso*, *"submit"*) is used for the attitude of the slave to the master as for that of wife to husband (v. 5) reflects the legal authority of the *paterfamilias*. At the same time, in both cases the writer is careful to specify that they are to be submissive to their own husbands/masters. What is in view is not the submissiveness of women or slaves as a class, but, once again, the good order of each individual household – it being taken for granted that such depended on the authority of the *paterfamilias* being properly recognized. As in 1 Tim. 6:1-2, nothing is said of the responsibility of the master (cf. Col. 4:1), but here that is paralleled by nothing's being said about the responsibility of the husband or the father. For some reason the writer restricts his counsel to one side of each of the three relationships that made up the typical household.

The goal of the slave should be to please the master; "*in everything*" could be linked to the first instruction, thus "*submissive in everything*" (NIV), or to the second, thus "*well-pleasing in everything*" (NRSV). Since the adjective "*well-pleasing*," "*acceptable*" (εὐάρεστος *euarestos*) is usually used in reference to God, we may assume that what is in view is the ideal slave (not one who pleases an evil master). He or she should not speak against or contradict the master (again as summing the ideal master; cf. 1 Tim. 2:11-12). Nor should the ideal slave misappropriate or pilfer (νοσφίζω *nosphizo*) anything from the master (cf. Acts 5:2-3). These last two words give a sharp insight into the temptations typically confronting the slave and to which, no doubt, many succumbed. The Christian alternative was to "*show/demonstrate all faithfulness as good*"; the Christian slave should be the ideal slave. Such behavior would "*adorn/to ornament*" (κοσμέω *kosmeo*; cf. 1 Tim. 2:9) the teaching of the Savior in every way. Once again the concern is prominent that the Christian message should produce behavior that would commend it to others.

Excursus #5: *Haustafel*

The German word *"Haustafel"* (*"house table"*) refers to a summary table of specific actions members of each domestic pair in a household are expected to perform. *"Haustafel"* is also known as the New Testament *"Household Codes,"* consists of instructions in the New Testament writings to pairs of Christian people in different domestic and civil structures of society. The main foci of the Household Codes are upon husband/wife, parent/child, and master/slave relationship. The Codes apparently were developed to urge the new 1st century Christians to comply with the non-negotiable requirements of Roman *Patria Potestas* law, and to meet the needs for order within the fledgling churches. The two main passages that explain these relationships and duties are Ephesians 5:22-6:9 and Colossians 3:18-4:1. An underlying Household Code is also reflected in 1 Timothy 2:1-8, 3:1-8, 5:16, 6:1; Titus 2:1-10 and 1 Peter 2:13-3:7.

Historically, *"proof texts"* (the practice of using isolated, out of context quotations) from the New Testament Household Codes – from the 1st century to the present day – have been used to subordinate married Christian women to their husbands, and to disqualify women from primary ministry positions in Christian churches.

Titus 2:11~15 → Theological Basis: The Appearance of Christ

NIV	TT
[11] For the grace of God has appeared that offers salvation to all people. [12] It teaches us to say "No" to ungodliness and worldly passions, and to live self-controlled, upright and godly lives in this present age, [13] while we wait for the blessed hope—the appearing of the glory of our great God and Savior, Jesus Christ, [14] who gave himself for us to redeem us from all wickedness and to purify for himself a people that are his very own, eager	[11] For the **grace**[28] of God has **appeared**,[29] bringing **salvation**[30] to all, [12] **training**[31] us to renounce **ungodly**[32] and **worldly**[33] desires, and in the present age to live lives that are self-controlled, upright, and godly, [13] while we wait for the blessed hope and the manifestation of the glory of our great **God**[34] and **Savior**,[35] Jesus Christ. [14] He it is who gave himself for us from all iniquity and purify for himself a people of his own who are zealous for

---

[28] χάρις {khar-ece} → It means "*grace*," "*delight*," "*favor*," "*pleasure*," "*goodwill*," and "*credit*."

[29] ἐπιφαίνω {ep-eefah-ee-no} → It means "*appear*," "*give light*," "*become visible*," "*to become clearly known*," and "*to show one's self*."

[30] σωτήριον {so-tay-ree-on} → It means "*saving*," "*salvation*," and "*delivering*."

[31] παιδεύω {paideuo} → It means "*instruct*," "*train*," "*educate*," "*correct*," "*give guidance to*," "*discipline with punishment*," "*whip*," and "*scourge*."

[32] ἀσέβεια {as-ebi-ah} → It means "*impiety*," "*ungodliness*," and "*ungodly*."

[33] κοσμικός {kos-mee-kos} → It means "*worldly*," "*earthly*," and "*belonging to the world*."

[34] θεός {the-os} → It means "*a god or goddess*," "*the Godhead*," "*God the Father*," "*a deity*," and "*the supreme Divinity*."

[35] σωτήρ {so-tare} → It means "*savior*," "*deliverer*," and "*preserver*."

to do what is good.	good deeds.
¹⁵ These, then, are the things you should teach. Encourage and rebuke with all authority. Do not let anyone despise you.	¹⁵ **Declare**³⁶ these things; exhort and reprove with all authority. Let no one look down on you.

What follows, in effect, is another faithful saying – that is, a summary of the gospel (vv.11-14). In focuses on the coherence between the two appearing of Christ (vv.11, 13), between what has already been accomplished (vv.11, 14) and the hope for what is yet to happen (v.13). It is this correlation that provides the rationale for godly living in the present (v.12), as illustrated by the preceding paragraph. The exposition is completed with a repetition of the commission to Titus (v.15), the section as a whole (vv.1-15) being held together by the two bracketing exhortations (v.1 and v.15).

- **11 – 15** The opening of the theological affirmation (v. 11) is very similar to that of 2 Tim. 1:9-10, with the common talk of the generous "*grace/favor*" of God and its saving manifestation. The language echoes traditional talk of God's self-revelation (as at Bethel in Gen. 35:7 and in the Temple in *2 Macc.* 3:30). Christ is not mentioned as such, and, unusually, it is the adjective (rather than verb or noun) that is used: "*bringing salvation.*" But even if it is not clear enough here, the parallel between the two passages puts it beyond dispute that what is in view is the grace of God

---

³⁶ λαλέω {la-leo} → It means "*to sound,*" "*to speak,*" "*to proclaim,*" "*to declare,*" "*to utter,*" and "*to preach.*"

enacted in and through Christ in his first appearing. As in 1 Tim. 2:3-4 and 4:10, it is assumed that the purpose of God's gracious action in Christ is the salvation of all.

The immediate switch to first-person plural (*"training us"*) is not a sudden diminution of that universal goal to the few who have responded. Rather, it is a reminder that the training of the few has in view the salvation of the whole (v. 12). Not that the few are envisaged as shock troops or as some elite squad charged to complete the saving purpose of God for all. Rather, the thought seems to be of the few as the first colony or circle of salvation, who by living as those on the way to complete salvation function as a representative sample of humanity, whose very life style will be a witness to the quality of God's saving purpose. This is presumably why this final paragraph can function as the theological rationale for the seemingly mundane household rules of vv. 1-10. It is divine grace expressed in the quality of basic human relationships that will be the most effective witness to the character of God's saving purpose.

For the same reason, the point of the earlier manifestation of God's grace can be put in such simple terms as *"educating," "training," "disciplining"* (v. 12) the word "παιδεύω" (*paideuo*) embracing all that was involved in a good upbringing. The negative and positive goals of this education are both summed up in familiar Pastoral terms: "refusing/repudiating ungodliness" and *"living a godly life in the present age."* The former is elaborated in terms of worldly desires; there is a fine distinction involved here between "*κοσμιος*" (*kosmios*), denoting what society would respect (cf. 1 Tim. 2:9), and "*κοσμικὰς*" (*kosmilkos*), denoting what partook too much of the world in its opposition to God – that is, desires becoming lusts, desires for advancement and gain in the world. The latter is elaborated with the adverbial form of the term already used three times in the letter as an adjective (σωφρόν, *sophron*), "*soberly moderately/ displaying self-control*," as well as with the adverbial form of its partner in 1:8 (δικαίως, *dikaios*), "*justly.*" The appearance of three of the most highly prized virtues in Greek thought (piety, moderation, justice), following the classic Greek term for education, underlies the degree to which the Christianity of the Pastorals saw itself as complementary to the highest aspirations of Greek philosophical ethics. The resulting picture is not very dynamic, but what is in view is the character of responsible living and relationships as the most potent forces of all.

What gives the community its dynamism is more the hope of what is to come; the community literally lives in hope of the appearance of Christ (v.13). Indicative of the character of Christian hope is the fact that the word is used here for what is hoped for (cf. Col. 1:5). Hope does not depend on human feelings of hopefulness, but on the one in whom that hope is invested. This is the second "*appearing*" in view, and, as with the first (v. 11), the theme of "*salvation*" (here "*Savior*") is linked with it (cf. 2 Tim. 1:10). Clearly implied, then, is the thought that salvation is a process from first to second, begun by Christ's saving act in the first (v. 14) and climaxed by his appearing again. This also helps to clarify why the title "*Savior*" can be used equally of God and of Christ, for it is the saving purpose of God (v. 11) that is brought to effect in both appearing.

Verse 13 is particularly interesting for its Christology, for the blessed hope is expressed as "*the appearance of the glory of our great God and Savior Jesus Christ.*" The interest is not just in the further example of Christ being called "*Savior.*" It focuses more on the preceding phrase. Almost certainly what is in view is not a double appearance (of God and of Christ) – that would be a less obvious rendering of the Greek, and the formula "*God and Savior*" was common in inscriptions of the time. The point is, rather, that Christ is described by the whole phrase: "*our great God and Savior.*" In other words, here we have one of very few instances in the New Testament where Christ is called "*God*" (otherwise only John 1:1, 18; 20:28; Heb. 1:8; and possibly Rom. 9:5). This is how most understand the phrase. But it is also possible that it is the still fuller phrase that should be taken in apposition to Jesus Christ: "*the glory of our great God and Savior*" – that is, Christ described as the visible manifestation of divine glory (as in John 12:41, referring to Isa. 6:10). Either way, the passage becomes a clear measure of the amazing significance already recognized in or attributed to Christ, that in Christ Christians realize that God, insofar as God may be known to human beings, had been manifested.

Just as the hope of the second appearing rests on the first, so also the recognition of Christ's divine significance rests on what he has already done (v. 14). The language of v. 14a is that of already well-established summaries of the gospel and is very similar to that of 1 Tim. 2:6. There is a strong echo of Ps. 130:8; The Lord "*will redeem Israel from all his iniquities.*" That the echo is deliberate is confirmed by the talk of God's cleansing "*a chosen people, a people of his own*" (cf. Exod. 19:5; Deut. 7:6; 14:2; Ezek. 37:23). Clearly, then, the thought is of these little Christian communities in Crete fulfilling God's purpose for Israel. As Israel was pledged to live as God's people, so these Christians should be "*zealous for good works.*" Given the hostility to "*those of the circumcision*" and to "*Jewish myths*" (Titus 1:10, 14), this positive assertion of the continuity of Israel in the Christian churches of Crete should be noted. And since the thought is of a piece with that of God as Savior of all (Titus 2:11), the implication presumably is that the churches, like Israel, formed a representative people, chosen with a view to benefit all, to be a light to the nations (cf. Isa. 49:1-16).

This, it should be noted again, is the rationale for the preceding instruction on good household management (vv. 1-10): Israel's obligation to be a people dedicated to God, living lives and maintaining households of positive benefit to neighbor and community. The repetition of the opening command (v. 1) in the final sentence (v. 15) underscores the integration of the whole chapter, with the "*sound *teaching*" (v. 1) now documented both in its theological rationale (vv. 11-14) and in its practical outworking (vv 2-10), and providing Titus with the terms of reference for both encouragement and reproof, as also the authority behind both (cf. 1 Tim. 4:12).

Titus 3:1~2 → Instruction to the Whole Church

NIV	TT
3 [1] Remind the people to be subject to rulers and authorities, to be obedient, to be ready to do whatever is good, [2] to slander no one, to be peaceable and considerate, and always to be gentle toward everyone.	**3** [1] **Remind**[37] them to be **subject**[38] to (legitimate) rulers, to be obedient, and ready for every good works, [2] to speak evil about no one, to be peaceful, balanced, and **showing**[39] complete gentleness toward everyone.

After the summary description of Titus' task and the word of personal encouragement (cf. Titus 2:15), the author gives a detailed analysis of the kind of exhortation that Titus is expected to use in addressing the congregation. Titus is urged to explain to the congregation just what is meant by *"good works."*

- **1 – 2** Using five infinitives, the author has constructed a list of seven virtues to illustrate the meaning of the phrase. These infinitives are dependent upon an initial hortatory *"remind them."* The reminder serves as an indication that Cretan believers were supposed to have been aware of these things even before Titus began his work of pastoral exhortation among them.

---

[37] ὑπομιμνῄσκω {hoop-om-im-nace-ko} → It means *"to cause one to remember,"* *"bring to remembrance,"* *"recall to mind,"* *"remind,"* *"bring up,"* and *"put in mind."*

[38] ὑποτάσσω {hoop-to-asso} → It means *"to subordinate,"* *"to subject,"* *"obey,"* *"to submit to one's control,"* and *"be subject."*

[39] ἐνδεικνυμένους {endei-kny-menous} → It means *"show,"* *"demonstrate,"* *"do,"* *"appoint,"* and *"designate."*

Respect for legitimate authority and obedience is cited as the first of the Christian's social responsibilities. The expression *"rulers, authorities"* without any conjunction, seems best rendered by *"(legitimate) rulers,"* that is, rulers who are able to exercise authority over their subjects. Both words occur in the Pastorals only here. It is not unlikely that the author's words are intended to be a reminder that Christians should avoid any kind of evil disobedience that would render them suspect in the eyes of governmental authorities and perhaps lead to violence or some other form of persecution (cf. 1 Pet. 2:13-15). 1 Tim. 2:1-2 urges the members of the community to pray for kings and all people in authority *"so that we might live a peaceful and quiet life in all godliness and dignity."* Obedience to civil authorities serves to enhance the community in the eyes of those outside, protects them against oppression, and creates the circumstances that enable them to enjoy a certain quality of life.

In addition to their civic responsibilities, Christians must be *"ready for every good work"* (cf. 2 Tim. 2:21; 3:17). In contrast, those who have not been purified are unsuitable for every good work (cf. Titus 1:16). *"Every good work"* is the Christian life in its totality. The adjective *"every"* must be taken distributively to include every sort of good work.

The author expands the general exhortation with a series of remarks that indicate that members of the chosen people should have good social graces. They are to speak evil of no one. In addition, they are to embrace a triad of virtues that are necessary for a good social life; they are to be peaceful, fair, and gentle with regard to everyone. The author's emphasis on "*all*" and "*none*" may reflect the paraenetic genre. The genre consists of general exhortations rather than specific directions. Thus, believers are urged to speak maliciously about no one at all, and to be peaceful, balanced, and gentle toward everyone. It may be, however, that "*toward everyone*" is a salient qualification. The author might have been concerned lest civil authorities (cf. 1 Tim. 2:1) and outsiders be excluded from the Christian's social outreach. In any case, the participle "*ἐνδεικνυμένους*," "*showing*" is taken from the world of rhetoric. Its literal meaning is to "*demonstrate*," indicating that the fully lived ethical life has a demonstrative appeal. Appropriate social behavior on the part of believers serves as an argument in favor of their faith.

Members of the chosen people are to exclude no one from his or her social-mindedness. Using a familiar triadic mode – the two adjectives and the participle are controlled by the verb "*to be*" (εἶναι) – the author describes the believer's interaction with others as characterized by a calm peacefulness, fairness, and gentleness. All three virtues figured in Hellenistic descriptions of life in society: the absence of contentiousness by Aechylus, balance by Herodotus, and gentleness by Plato and other Greek authors. The first two of these virtues are among those expected to be found in the life of a person who is qualified to serve as an overseer of the house of God (cf. 1 Tim. 3:3).

Titus 3:3~8 → Theological Basis: Conversion & Baptism

NIV	TT
[3] At one time we too were foolish, disobedient, deceived and enslaved by all kinds of passions and pleasures. We lived in malice and envy, being hated and hating one another. [4] But when the kindness and love of God our Savior appeared, [5] he saved us, not because of righteous things we had done, but because of his mercy. He saved us through the washing of rebirth and renewal by the Holy Spirit, [6] whom he poured out on us	[3] For at one time we were **ignorant**[40], **disobedient**[41], going astray, enslaved to various passions and pleasures, living in evil and jealousy, despicable and hateful of one another. [4] When appeared the **goodness**[42] and **benevolence**[43] of our Savior, God, [5] not from works of righteousness that we ourselves have done, but according to his mercy, he saved us through the washing of **rebirth**[44] and **renewal**[45] by the Holy Spirit, [6] which he poured out on us

---

[40] ἀνόητοι {ano-ay-tos} → It means *"not understood," "fool," "unwise," "foolish," "unintelligible," "ignorant,"* and *"senseless."*

[41] ἀπειθεῖς {ap-i-thace} → It means *"impersuasible," "disobedient," "not compliant,"* and *"contumacious."*

[42] χρηστότης {khray-stot-ace} → It means *"moral goodness," "integrity," "benignity," "kindness," "gentleness,"* and *"goodness."*

[43] φιλανθρωπία {filan-thro-pia} → It means *"love for humanity," "kindness," "generosity," "hospitality,"* and *"benevolence."*

[44] παλιγγενεσία {pal-ling-ghen-esseeah} → It means *"new birth," "reproduction," "renewal," "recreation,"* and *"regeneration."*

[45] ἀνακαίνωσις {anakah-ee-no-sis} → It means *"renewal," "renovation,"* and *"complete change for the better."*

generously through Jesus Christ our Savior, [7] so that, having been justified by his grace, we might become heirs having the hope of eternal life. [8] This is a trustworthy saying. And I want you to stress these things, so that those who have trusted in God may be careful to devote themselves to doing what is good. These things are excellent and profitable for everyone.	profusely through Jesus Christ, our Savior, [7] so that, justified by his grace, we may become heirs according to the hope of eternal life. [8] This is a trustworthy saying. I want you to **insist**[46] on all these things so that those who have come to believe in God **make every effort**[47] to choose good works. These are things that are good and beneficial for **human beings**[48].

By way of further explanation (γάρ) of the kind of life that members of the chosen people are to lead, the pastor contrasts the way that they are now expected to live (vv. 1-2) with the way that they once lived. They have a conversion experience.

The vocabulary and rhythm of the hymn indicate that it was a preexistent unit that the author has employed and on which he has already offered a kind of commentary (Titus 2:11-14). It is not only the internal evidence of the hymn that suggests that it is borrowed material; the author himself says as much when he qualifies the hymn as "*a trustworthy saying.*" The hymn contains one of the most

---

[46] διαβεβαιόομαι {dee-abebahee-o-omahee} → It means "*to affirm strongly*," "*affirm*," "*assert confidently*," "*speak confidently*," and "*insist*."

[47] φροντίζω {fron-tid-zo} → It means "*to think*," "*to be careful*," "*to be thoughtful*," "*to be anxious*," and "*concerned*."

[48] ἄνθρωπος {an-thro-pos} → It means "*human being*," "*person*," "*man*," "*husband*," "*humanity*," and "*son*."

important statements on the nature of baptism to be found in the New Testament (cf. Rom. 6:3-11).

The reference in the hymn to the Holy Spirit is one of only two explicit mentions of the Spirit in the Pastoral Epistles (cf. 2 Tim. 1:14). As did the prior epiphany passage, the hymn situates the existence of the Christian between two appearances of Jesus Christ. Its dominant theme is salvation, effected by Jesus Christ and imparted to Christians in the baptismal ritual. The ritual enables the baptized to be heirs, hoping for eternal life.

- **3** The author's use of the *"once-now"* scheme reflects early Christian usage (once heathen, now illumined or cleansed, cf. Titus 3:3-7; Rom. 6:17-18; 7:5-6; 11:20-32; Gal. 4:3-9; 1 Cor. 6:9-11; Col. 3:5-10; Eph. 2:1-10, 11-13; 1 Pet. 2:25; 4:3-4; once hidden, now revealed, in Titus 1:2-3; 2 Tim. 1:9-10; Rom. 16:25-27; 1 Cor. 2:7-10; Col. 1:26-27; Eph. 3:5-6; 8-10; 1 Pet. 1:20).

  Occasionally this outline is employed in a portrayal of the history of salvation. Once salvation was hidden; now it has been revealed. At other times, the outline is used to contrast humankind under the influence of sin with humankind redeemed. This is the contrast between the *"old person"* and the *"new person."* In 1 Tim. 1:12-17 the *"once-now"* scheme is used to describe Paul's conversion. In Titus 3:3 it is used to contrast the life of believers with the life of those who have not yet or will never receive baptismal regeneration (cf. Titus 3:3-7). The author's contrasting explanation offers a qualifying nuance to what he has just enjoined upon Titus. Titus is to *"remind them"* (Titus 3:1) of how they should live. He is to remind them of their baptismal catechesis.

As is typical when the *"once-now"* scheme is used to describe two conditions of a human being, the author employs a catalog of vices to describe what life was like before baptism. His list contains eight vices. The first two, *"ignorant"* and *"disobedient,"* are expressed in terms that use a privative alpha, "ἀνόητοι" (*a-noetoi*) and "ἀπειθεῖς" (*a-peitheis*). Christians were people who once lacked intelligence and the spirit of obedience (cf. Titus 1:16). The former description speaks derisively of their former state. While the term *"ignorant"* may allude to the fact that prior to baptism Christians were ignorant of the message of the gospel (*"the full knowledge of truth"*) and its demands, the term was commonly used to describe someone who was witless, foolish, stupid, and silly.

Their former disobedience contrasts with the obedience that is now expected of them. Earlier they were led astray; now they are presumed to be on the right path. The vocabulary that the author uses to identify the third vice on his list reflects the language of Hellenistic moral discourse. *"Don't go astray"* was a popular moral exhortation (cf. Epictetus, *Discourses* 4.623; 1 Cor. 6:9; 15:33; Gal. 6:7). A popular Stoic proverb spoke of those who had gone astray leading others astray (cf. 2 Tim. 3:13). One could be led astray by all sorts of things – desire, sensuality, the lure of external things, unclear ideas, and false teaching.

According to Plato, someone who goes astray is lacking in purpose and virtue (cf. *Republic* 9.586a). The one who has gone astray simply leads an aimless life.

The author shares with the philosophic moralists of his day the concern that Christians not live a life of sensuality. For the stoics, the ideal of the moral life was a life without passion. Influenced by this view, the author describes the former life of the members of the community as one that was enslaved to passions and various pleasures (cf. 1 Tim. 6:9).

The final phrases of the author's description of the former lifestyle of those social graces given in Titus 3:2. The author begins to describe their antisocial conduct with a participial phrase that depicts them having lived in evil and jealousy. The two phrases are arranged in a chiastic structure; encompassing participles embrace a pair of vices. Reflecting his Semitic tradition, Paul commonly described life as a journey, a walk. The Pastoral Epistles do not use the Pauline expression; rather, the author speaks of life as a passing through (cf. 1 Tim. 2:2), a verb used by Herodotus and other Hellenistic authors. As they passed through life prior to their baptism, believers lived a life of evil and jealousy. Neither term is found on Philo's long list of 146 vices in *Abel and Cain* 32. Such was the wide variety of terms from which Hellenistic authors were able to compile a list of vices.

The author's next two vices, *"despicable"* and *"hating one another"* likewise make no appearance on Philo's long list. Together the two terms mean *"being hated and hateful of others."* *"Despicable"* was used by such classical authors as Aeschylus (*Prometheus* 592), Philo (*Decalogue* 131), Clement (*1 Clem.* 35:6), and Heliodorus (5.29.4) in the sense of hated, abominable, or despicable. Echoing the language of the author's catalog of vices, Clement of Rome described the tormenters of Hananiah, Azariah, and Mishael as *"abominable men and full of all wickedness"* (cf. *1 Clem.* 45:7). The author notes that prior to baptism, the members of the community had been hateful to one another. This is the obvious antithesis of the Christian demand to love one another.

- **4 – 7** The hymn proclaims that the goodness and benevolence of our Savior, God (cf. Titus 1:3; 2:10), have appeared. Neither *"goodness"* nor *"benevolence"* occurs elsewhere in the Pastorals. The former is, nonetheless, a Pauline term (cf. Rom. 2:4; 3:12; 11:22; 2 Cor. 6:6; Gal. 5:22; Col. 3:12); the latter occurs elsewhere in the New Testament only in Acts 28:2. *"Goodness"* and *"benevolence"* are, however, a classic pair. Philo writes that the emperor Gaius had once been thought to be *"good and benevolent"* (cf. *Gaius* 67), showing fairness and fellowship to everyone. He argues with a hypothetical moneylender who outwardly shows goodness and benevolence (cf. *Special Laws* 2.75) while providing to be inhumane and brutal in his actions. He characterizes as a false goodness and benevolence (cf. *Special Laws* 3.156) a parental or filial piety that leads a father to be punished instead of his son, or a son to be punished instead of his father.

Josephus wrote that Gedaliah, appointed governor over the towns of Judea by the king of Babylon, showed such *"goodness and benevolence"* (*Ant.* 10.9.3) that Johanan and other leaders of the Jews (Jer. 40:8) experienced a great love for him. The physician Galen praised his father because of his benevolence and goodness. Dio Cassius (ca. 164-229 C.E.) wrote that *"a benevolence, a goodness, attentive care for everything that pertains to the public interest"* were qualities of the administration of the emperor Pertinax (*Roman History* 73.5.2). The philosopher Onasander wrote that a general should treat with benevolence and goodness cities that open their gates in surrender (*General* 18.1).

Benevolence was widely viewed as the quintessential quality of a good king. The Rosetta Stone lauds Ptolemy V, a benevolent ruler who had freely given away all the money that belonged to him (Rosetta Stone 12). The good king is prepared to show clemency to the conquered (Plutarch, *Cicero* 21.4) and to shower benefits on the people so that harmony and peace might reign in the kingdom (*P. Lond.* 1912.102). The quality of royal benevolence included the duty not to inflict punishment too readily or to increase people's sufferings (*Ep. Arist.* 208). Hellenistic papyri offer many examples of petitions addressed to kings or their legates by people who appeal to their benevolence as they ask these royals to intervene in a given situation. Kings who showed benevolence expected that their subjects would show benevolence and love in return (*Ep. Arist.* 265). Several papyri show that in fact people were thanked for their benevolence (*P. Mich.* 483.3; *P. Oxy.* 3057.8).

In sum, manifestations of goodness and benevolence were to be expected when a king, his governor, or his general arrived for a solemn visit to a city. Evidence of such goodness and benevolence manifested that the arriving personage was indeed a Savior or benefactor. Since the royal sovereign was often considered to be a representative of the deity – sometimes to the point of being *"divinized"* himself – these expressions of goodness and benevolence were manifestations of the goodness and benevolence of the gods. Philo attributed benevolence to God, the king of kings, who deigns to visit human beings (*Cherubim* 99). In Philo's view, benevolence is a divine attribute. It belongs to the very nature of God (*Moses* 1.198). God manifests his benevolence in order to show honor to the ruler that he had appointed.

The first verse of the author's hymn captures this rich Hellenistic image of the formal arrival of an emperor or god. The Hellenistic world associated the benevolence manifested on these solemn occasions with clemency. Philo links both clemency (*Moses* 1.198) and tender mercy (*Cherubim* 99) with the royal and divine attribute of benevolence. In similar fashion the author's baptismal hymn associates the manifestation of God's goodness and benevolence with his mercy. Mercy, a gift of God (cf. 1 Tim. 1:2; 2 Tim. 1:2, 16, 18), is contrasted with works of righteousness that we ourselves have done. The emphatic pronoun *"we ourselves"* highlights the contrast between what we have done and what God manifests.

"*Works of righteousness*" has a Pauline ring, but the apostle did not actually use the phrase "*in righteousness.*" Writing about righteousness or justification, Paul occasionally used a prepositional phrase that includes "*righteousness*" as the object of the preposition, but the preposition is either "*ειϲ*" "*in,*" following Gen. 15:6 LXX (cf. Rom. 4:3, 5, 9, 22; 6:16; 10:4, 10; Gal. 3:6), or "*διὰ*" "*through,*" "*on account of*" (cf. Rom. 4:13; 5:21; 8:10). The prepositional phrase used by the author is, however, found in four pseudepigraphic epistles, all influenced in some degree by the writings of Paul (cf. Titus 3:5; 2 Tim. 3:16; Eph. 4:24; 2 Pet. 1:1). This nondescript phrase echoes Paul's language but reflects none of the verve of his argument.

The phrase "*justified by his grace,*" on the other hand, reflects Paul's thoughts as it took shape in discussions with those "*Judaizers*" who troubled Christian communities in Rome and Galatia. Human beings are justified not by their own efforts but by the justifying gift of God. The hymn's double reference to righteousness (vv. 5, 7) captures and emphasizes, by means of its inherent contrast, the apostle's conviction that we are not justified by our own works; rather, we are justified by the saving grace of God. Recollection of this Pauline notion is apropos in a document purportedly intended for Christians living in a society where there were considerable numbers of Jews and the Christian community itself had to deal with various matters pertaining to Judaism (cf. Titus 1:10, 14-15).

Encompassing as they do the formulaic "*according to his mercy*," the hymn's two references to righteousness provide a setting for and a Pauline clarification of the notion of the Savior's mercy. In the Hellenistic world, mercy, judgment, and benevolence were qualities that one expected to find in a judge (cf. Demosthenes, *Against Meidias* 21.100; Plato, *Apology* 34c, 35b). As one might appeal to a sovereign's benevolence, so might one appeal to a judge's mercy (Plato, *Apology* 34c) and be thankful when mercy was rendered (*P. Magd.* 18.6). Mercy was apposite to the pursuit of justice.

According to the Hebrew Scriptures (cf. Num. 14:18; Joel 2:13; Ps. 86:5, 15) and early Christian writings, the mercy of God is a give (cf. 1 Tim. 1:2; 2 Tim. 1:2). The author explains that God's mercy is realized in the salvation that we receive through baptism by the Holy Spirit, with the result that we are justified by grace and become heirs. In the hymn, the Savior's mercy is not only cast in the light of the Pauline understanding of justification, and contrasted with such righteous works as are done by humans; it is also explained in terms of salvation itself. Our Savior, God, motivated by mercy, has saved us. The Savior is one from whom salvation is expected; the Savior is also one who has already saved us.

This the Savior has done by means of "*the washing of rebirth and renewal by the Holy Spirit*." The word "*washing*" renders a Greek term (cf. Eph. 5:26) that variously designates a bath, the water with which one bathes, or the act of washing. The act of washing is a common act of human hygiene. From time immemorial, however, washing has served as a ritual action. Ceremonial washings whether of the whole body or of particular parts of the body, were sometimes a rite of passage, symbolizing the passage from one state in life to another. At other times, ceremonial ablutions symbolized the transition from the secular to the sacred (cf. *EncRel* 1.9-13). A ritual bathing of the entire body served as an initiation ceremony for Jewish proselytes. In the Eleusinian mysteries, the rite of initiation, held during the February celebrations of the Lesser Mysteries at Agrai, concluded with a ritual washing in which water was poured over the initiate. The ceremonies at Agrai were a prelude to the September celebrations of the Greater Mysteries at Eleusis. Among Christians, bodily immersion into water (baptism) was the rite of entrance into the Christian community.

The ritual bath mentioned in the hymn is one of rebirth and renewal. The term "παλιγγενεσία" (rebirth) from "παλιν" (again) and "γενομαι" (to come into being, birth) occurs elsewhere in the New Testament only in Matt. 19:28. The term was commonly used in the Hellenistic world of a wide range of human or metahuman experiences, including the restoration of health, return from exile, the beginning of a new life, the restoration of souls, new life for a people, and the anticipated restoration of the world.

The *Corpus Hermeticum*, an Alexandrian text written sometime before the end of the 3rd century C.E.

and attributed to the *"Thrice-Greatest Hermes"* (Hermes Trismegistos), says that *"no one can be saved before rebirth"* (*Corp. Herm.* 13.3). The thirteenth tract of the Corpus features a dialogue between Hermes and his son Tat on the subject of being born again. Speaking to his father in a manner that recalls Nicodemus' question to Jesus (cf. John 3:4), Tat inquires about rebirth. He understands rebirth to be accomplished in some physical manner and asks his father about the womb and seed. Hermes responds that these are respectively the wisdom of understanding in silence and the true good, sown in a person by the will of God. The child that results is a different kind of child, *"a god and a child of God"* (*Corp. Herm.* 13.2). Rebirth enables a person to progress in the moral life, turning from twelve vices – ignorance, grief, incontinence, lust, injustice, greed, deceit, envy, treachery, anger, recklessness, and malice – to the opposite virtues (*Corp. Herm.* 13.7).

Many 20th century scholars, particularly those belonging to the history of religion school of New Testament research, attempted to clarify 3:5 in the light of this Hermetic tract. The tract is, however, much later than the Letter to Titus and lacks any reference to a ritual washing. On the other hand, the late 1st century canonical Fourth Gospel features a discourse between Jesus and Nicodemus, a leader of the Pharisees (John 3:3-8), about being *"born again."* The Johannine account does not employ the noun *"rebirth"* (παλιγγενεσία), as does the *Corpus*, but it does speak about a birth that takes place in water and the Spirit.

The substantive similarities between the Johannine text and Titus 3:5 – the references to washing, new birth, and the Spirit – suggest that both of these late 1st century texts describe the ritual of Christian baptism as bringing about a new life through the power of the Holy Spirit.

The author explains what he means by rebirth by adding "*and renewal by the Holy Spirit.*" The ritual ablution of baptism effects a rebirth that is also a renewal. Elsewhere in the New Testament, the term "*renewal*" appears only in Rom. 12:2, the first attested usage of a term that appears only in Christian literature. Apart from these two New Testament passages, the term is found in *Herm. Vis.* 3.8.9, where the female figure speaks to Hermas about "*the renewal of your spirits.*" This phrase connotes the conversion that is necessary as the eschaton approaches. Throughout the New Testament, the word "*new*" generally has an eschatological connotation. The Pastoral Epistles evoke the eschatological future when they use "*epiphany*" language to speak of the future appearance of the great God and Savior, Jesus Christ (cf. 1 Tim. 6:14; 2 Tim. 4:1, 8; Titus 2:13).

In his commentary on the opening lines of this hymn (Titus 2:11-12), the author explained what baptismal conversion entails. It is a matter of denying impiety and worldly passions. It is living modestly, justly, and piously while we wait in hope for the appearance of the glory of the great God and our Savior.

The new life and conversion associated with the baptismal washing result from the working of the Holy

Spirit. The Pastoral Epistles do not have a developed pneumatology. It is only here and in 2 Tim. 1:14 that explicit reference is made to the Holy Spirit, the power of God at work. Early Christian tradition, however, generally associates baptism and its effects with the work of the Holy Spirit. The hymn reflects this tradition and its understanding that the Holy Spirit is the eschatological Spirit of God already at work in the present age. That the Holy Spirit effects a rebirth and a renewal is consistent with the biblical idea that the Spirit of God was at work in the creation of the universe and the creation of humankind (cf. Gen. 1-2). God's eschatological power effects a rebirth and a renewal.

The image of the pouring of water in the baptismal ritual continues to be evoked when the hymn speaks about the gift of the Holy Spirit that God *"has profusely poured"* out upon us. *"Profusely"* indicates the abundance and lavishness of God's gift of the Spirit. The idea that Jesus is the mediator of the gift of the Spirit in baptism is traditional (cf. John 1:26-27; 4:10, 14; 20:22-23; Luke 3:16; Mark 1:8; Matt. 3:11). The Johannine tradition particularly emphasizes the lavishness of this water gift and its relevance to eternal life (cf. John 4:14-15).

The New Testament expresses the idea of inheritance that the hymn associates with baptism. The inheritance motif does not otherwise appear in the Pastoral Epistles, but Paul often wrote about the inheritance, especially in Romans, 1 Corinthians, and Galatians. The idea of an inheritance is often linked, especially in Paul, with the notions of children of God, the Spirit, and baptism (cf. Rom. 8:14-17). The hymn's idea that those who are justified by grace are heirs is consistent with these Pauline ideas and with the post-Pauline notion that the seal of the promised Holy Spirit is the pledge of our inheritance (cf. Eph. 1:13-14). The very idea of an inheritance is forward looking. An inheritance is something that a person will receive in the future. Baptism is the guarantee that there will be an inheritance in the future. This inheritance is *"eternal life,"* a cipher for eschatological salvation in the author's circles.

▪ **8** The author places a seal of approval on his version of the baptismal hymn by adding, as a kind of final "amen,' the aphorism *"This is a trustworthy saying"* (see Excursus #6: "This is a trustworthy saying"). This use of his circles' stock phrase (cf. 1 Tim. 1:15; 3:1; 4:9; 2 Tim. 2:11) affirms that the unit he has just cited has faithfully reproduced the tradition handed down to him.

Excursus #6: "This is a trustworthy saying"

The words of the trustworthy sayings are message of faith, creedal cameos. In the Pastoral Epistles the sayings function in much the same way as do the creedal formulae of Paul's letters and the creeds of the later church. The leader of the community, the overseer, is to maintain these trustworthy sayings so that he can encourage the community and confront its opponents (Titus 1:9). Confirmation of the creedal nature of the faithful sayings can be found in the confessional *"that,"* which introduces the words *"Christ Jesus came into the world to save sinners"* in 1 Tim. 1:15. The verse could be translated,

---

"This is a faithful saying, worthy of full acceptance, that Christ Jesus came into the world to save sinners." It may have been that the community responded *"Amen!"* or even repeated *"This is a trustworthy saying"* (Πιστὸς ὁ λόγος) after hearing a formulation of faith introduced by *"This is a trustworthy saying."*

In some of the cases, the formula of trustworthiness is used with wording so terse that the words to which the formula is attached appear to have been a fixed formulation themselves. In this kind of formulation, they could easily be transmitted from one person to another, one church to another, and from generation to generation within the church (cf. 1 Tim. 1:15; 2 Tim. 2:11-13) or society (1 Tim. 4:9). In other instances the ideas endorsed may be traditional, but their formulation derives from the author. This would be the case in 1 Tim. 3:1 and Titus 3:8, two instances of the Pastorals' use of the shorter formula. In such instances the community is invited to accept the authority of the author as a reliable interpreter of tradition.

Used either to introduce or to ratify a traditional formula of faith, the formula functioned in much the same way as did the Hebrew *"Amen."* In Jewish culture, as both the canonical New Testament and the Qumran scrolls evidence, *"Amen"* was sometimes used to highlight the importance of a statement to follow or as an affirmation of the reliability of what had just been said. The single *"Amen"* of Jesus' discourse in the Synoptic Gospels (cf. Matt. 5:18) and the double *"Amen"* of some of his discourse in the Fourth Gospel (cf. John 1:51) are examples of the introductory use of *"Amen."* The Book of Revelation provides evidence of *"Amen,"* even a double *"Amen"* used as a response (cf. Rev. 1:6; 7:12) or acclamation of affirmation (Rev. 5:14; 19:4; 22:20). Revelation 7:12 suggests that *"Amen"* was sometimes used both to introduce and to confirm, while Rev. 1:7 provides evidence that the confirmatory *"Amen"* was sometimes duplicated. In the author's community, *"This is a trustworthy saying"* appears to have been used in much the same way.

What then do the words of the long formula *"worthy of full acceptance"* add to the familiar *"This is a trustworthy saying"*? The additional wording appears only in 1 Tim. 1:15 and 4:9, the only passages in the New Testament where the word *"acceptance"* is used. Hellenistic writers used the phrase *"worthy of acceptance"* to suggest that particular people or things were particularly worthy of approbation or admiration. Hierocles used the expression *"worthy of much acceptance"* (Stobaeus, *Anthology* 4.27.20) to describe some laws. Ultimately, what *"worthy of full acceptance"* adds to *"trustworthy"* is repetition for the sake of emphasis, much as the author of the Book of Revelation uses *"vaí"* (*"yea"* or *"verily"*), in addition to the *"Amen"* of Rev. 1:7.

The author looks back on the things about which he has written and urges Titus to insist (cf. 1 Tim. 1:7) on them. *"Insist"* is a common word in Hellenistic paraenesis. Used by Aristotle (*Rhetoric* 2.13.1), Demosthenes (*On the Treaty with Alexander* 17.30), and Polybius (*Histories* 12.12.6), the verb suggests speaking with confidence and affirming the importance of what is being said. Titus is to speak in this way so that those who have been entrusted to his pastoral supervision (Titus 1:5) might pursue a life of good works.

The apostle frequently describes Christians as *"believers,"* using a present participle (cf. 1 Thess. 1:7). The author's phrase uses a perfect participle and cites the object of belief, God. Some translations exploit the perfect tense of the participle so as to imply that Titus' community consisted largely of Gentiles who had undergone a conversion experience and now believe in God (NRSV, JB, and NEB). Other translations exploit the perfect by suggesting continuity in faith (AV, RSV, RNAB). Some of the translations that attempt to reflect a contemporary idiom simply render the Greek as *"who believe in God"* (CEV).

The translation *"who have come to believe in God"* does not sufficiently reflect the connotations of *"faith"* found in the Pastorals. In these writings, *"faith"* evokes the content of faith rather than the existential relationship suggested by Paul's use of the term. This nuance is not absent from the author's identification of the members of the community as those who have come to believe in God. They have come to believe in God as the community understands that belief in God to be. Jews would have believed in God, but prior to their entrance into the community they would not have believed in God according to the community's understanding of faith in God.

Those who believe in God must be committed to doing *"good works*,' the author's standard description of correct behavior. The verb *"make every effort"* (φροντίζωσιν; cf. TLNT 3.467-69) is an epistolary term often found in the papyri in both private and official correspondence. It suggests taking something to heart and actively pursuing it until the task is completed, often with the implication that the person has a responsibility to do so. According to the author, the task at hand is a preferential option for good works, an active preference for correct ethical conduct (Titus 3:14).

The author underscores the importance of his and Titus' exhortation with a simple ethical affirmation: *"These are things that are good and beneficial for human beings."* Both terms are substantivized adjectives. The author's use of the word *"beneficial"* adds an element of rhetorical appeal, the argument from advantage, to his observation. The good is to be done because it is advantageous for human beings to do so.

Titus 3:9 → Controversies & Genealogies

NIV	TT
[9] But avoid foolish controversies and genealogies and arguments and quarrels about the law, because these are unprofitable and useless.	[9] Avoid **stupid**[49] **controversies,**[50] genealogies, divisions, and quarrels **about the law,**[51] because they are **useless**[52] and **stupid.**[53]

In Greek, verse 9 is an independent sentence. Genealogies refers here not to the family trees often found in the Old Testament, but to the fanciful but impressive interpretations of the Bible as later illustrated by those gnostics who found their mythological system in the Bible.

- **9** As for Titus himself, he is to avoid foolish controversies, genealogies, divisions, and quarrels about the law. The four are linked together with a repeated *"and"* (καὶ), represented by a comma in the translation, in an exhortation that substantively reappears in 2 Tim. 2:23. Titus and Timothy are urged to be keepers of the peace in their respective communities. Timothy is exhorted to *"avoid foolish and stupid arguments, knowing that they produce quarrels."* What distinguishes the exhortation

---

[49] μωρός {mo-ros} → lit means *"foolish," "stupid," "fool," "godless," "impious,"* and *"moron."*

[50] ζήτησις {zay'-tay-sis} → It means *"investigation," "controversial question," "controversy," "discussion,"* and *"debate."*

[51] νομικός {nomi-kos} → It means *"pertaining to the law," "one learned in the law," "about the law,"* and *"lawyer."*

[52] ἀνωφελής {ano-fel-ace} → It means *"unprofitable," "useless,"* and *"harmful."*

[53] μάταιος {ma-tai-os} → It means *"idle," "empty," "worthless," "foolish,"* and *"stupid."*

addressed to Titus from the one addressed to Timothy is that Titus is also urged to avoid genealogies, divisions, and disputes about the law.

This kind of vocabulary is rarely used in the New Testament. *"Genealogies"* appears elsewhere only in 1 Tim. 1:4. Plato (*Timaeus* 22a) and Polybius (*Histories* 9.2.1) argue against myths and genealogical lists. The author had expressed a concern lest members of the community become fascinated by Jewish myths (Titus 1:14). The kind of genealogies to which he makes reference in Titus 3:9 may well be the kinds of Jewish lists found in the Bible, rabbinic sources and the Dead Sea Scrolls. The adjective *"νομικός," "about the law,"* is not used as an adjective in any other New Testament passage. The legal disputes to which the author refers are undoubtedly disputes about the Jewish law.

"Divisions" is a term used by Paul, generally to designate a vice associated with jealousy (cf. Rom. 1:29; Rom. 13:13; 1 Cor. 3:3; 2 Cor. 12:20; Gal. 5:20; Phil. 1:15). Only in 1 Cor. 1:11 does Paul use the term to speak of divisions within the community. The presence of *"divisions"* in the author's list of things to be avoided by Titus suggests that the community might possibly splinter. Titus is urged to make every effort that it not do so. The mention of *"divisions"* between *"genealogies"* and *"quarrels about the law"* may suggest that the precarious situation to which Titus must respond is some kind of fragmentation due to the presence of Jews in his community (cf. Titus 1:14-15; 3:5, 7).

The author concluded the hortatory words intended for believers with a reflection on the beneficial nature of good works. He concludes his direct exhortation to Titus with words about the futility of the things that Titus is to avoid. Foolish arguments, genealogies, divisions, and quarrels about the law are simply useless and stupid. No advantage whatsoever is to be had in pursuing them.

Titus 3:10~11 → Final Warning

NIV	TT
[10] Warn a divisive person once, and then warn them a second time. After that, have nothing to do with them. [11] You may be sure that such people are warped and sinful; they are self-condemned.	[10] After a first and then a second admonition, avoid the **divisive person,**[54] [11] knowing that such a one is **perverted**[55], **sinful**[56], and **self-condemned**[57].

Taking a retrospective view, the author proceeds to sum up what he has written thus far, giving the reason why he has written as he has. The author warns Titus not to give in to any of the things that were troubling his flock. This warning and the author's emphasis on Titus' obligation to confront those who have strayed from the truth and healthy behavior confirms that the church for which this epistle was intended was undergoing some difficulty. The author urges that there be no compromise.

- **10 – 11** Although Titus is to avoid getting involved in quarrels and foolish arguments, he is nonetheless urged to do what he can to bring an errant member of the community to his or her senses and back to the

---

[54] αἱρετικός {hair-e-tee-kos} → It means *"factious," "causing divisions," "schismatic," "heretic,"* and *"a follower of a false doctrine."*

[55] ἐξέστραπται {exe-strap-tai} → It means *"be turned aside," "be perverted," "to change for the worse," "pervert,"* and *"corrupt."*

[56] ἁμαρτάνω {ham-ar-tano} → It means *"to be without a share in," "to miss the mark," "to err," "to wander from the law of God," "violate God's law," "trespass," "sin,"* and *"offend."*

[57] αὐτοκατάκριτος {ow-tok-at-ak-ree-tos} → It means *"self-condemned."*

community (cf. 2 Tim. 2:25-26). If these efforts do not meet with success, Titus is to shun the divisive person. The idea that a recalcitrant person is to be treated as an outcast after a first and second warning is similar to the discipline enjoined by Matt. 18:15-17. The author's language is that of Hellenistic paraenesis. *"Admonition,"* writes the Pseudo-Demetrius, *"is the instilling of sense in the person who is being admonished, and teaching him what should and should not be done"* (*Epistolary Types* 7).

Titus must admonish the divisive person not once but twice. Then he must act. Knowing that the divisive person is perverted and sinful, Titus must stay out of that person's way (cf. 1 Tim. 4:7; 5:11; 2 Tim. 2:23). The verb suggests a nuance of aversion or repudiation. Repudiation may entail the excommunication of the recalcitrant person. The author's circles were aware that Paul himself had sometimes favored excommunication as a way of dealing with a recalcitrant sinner (cf. 1 Tim. 1:18-20; 1 Cor. 5:5).

The person whom Titus is to avoid so radically is described in four ways. He or she is divisive, perverted, sinful, and self-condemned. In Stoic literature, the adjective *"divisive"* was used of people who caused divisions. Literally meaning *"to turn away from"* or *"to turn inside out,"* the verb *"ἐξέστραπται"* was used metaphorically to mean *"thoroughly confused"* or *"perverted."* The Greek verb *"to sin"* (ἁμαρτάνει) is rarely used in the Pastorals (only here and in 1 Tim. 5:20). In the Greek Bible, this verb renders the Hebrew

"אטח." Both the Greek and the Hebrew literally means *"to miss the mark,"* but were commonly used in the metaphorical, theological sense of *"sin."* Hellenists would have understood the term as describing the actions of someone who had done wrong or had failed in his or her purpose.

Finally, the person to be avoided is described as self-condemned, someone who has made a judgment against himself or herself. The adjective was rarely used in Greek. Apart from a single occurrence in a fragment of Philos' *Sacred Parallels*, the term is found only in Christian literature. Since 3:11 may be its earliest occurrence in Greek literature, it may have been the author himself who coined the word.

Titus 3:12~15 → Final Remarks & Benediction

NIV	TT
[12] As soon as I send Artemas or Tychicus to you, do your best to come to me at Nicopolis, because I have decided to winter there. [13] Do everything you can to help Zenas the lawyer and Apollos on their way and see that they have everything they need. [14] Our people must learn to devote themselves to doing what is good, in order to provide for urgent needs and not live unproductive lives. [15] Everyone with me sends you greetings. Greet those who love us in the faith. Grace be with you all.	[12] When I send Artemas or Tychicus to you, **make every effort**[58] to come to me at Nicopolis, for I have decided to spend the winter there. [13] Get **Zenas**[59], the lawyer, and Apollos ready and send them on their way. Make sure that they lack nothing that they need. [14] Let our people learn how to choose good works in situations of urgent need so that they are not **ineffective**[60]. [15] Everybody with me sends you greetings. Greet those who love us in faith. Grace be with all of you.

The final remarks in the epistle have the form of a kind of travelogue. It was not unusual for Paul to mention his travel plans in his letters. He frequently mentioned his

---

[58] σπούδασον {spoo-da-son} → It means *"hasten," "hurry," "be eager," "be zealous," "take pains," "make every effort," "be diligent," "be forward,"* and *"study."*

[59] Ζηνᾶς {Zay-nas} → The name means *"Jupiter."*

[60] ἄκαρπος {ak-ar-pos} → It means *"without fruit," "unfruitful," "useless," "unproductive,"* and *"ineffective."*

desire to visit those to whom he was writing (cf. Rom. 1:10-11; 15:22-24, 28-29; 1 Cor. 11:34; 16:3; 2 Cor. 1:15-16; 12:20-21; 13:10; Phil. 2:24; 1 Thess. 2:17-18; Phlm. 22). Toward the end of a letter, Paul occasionally entered into some detail about his travel plans (cf. Rom. 15:22-29; 1 Cor. 16:5-9). The author's mention of a port city and an allusion to the difficulty of winter travel are consistent with the literary genre. The epistle concludes with customary greetings in the first, second, and third persons – all of them tersely stated – but does not have the appended handwritten note found in some of Paul's own letters (cf. 1 Cor. 16:21; Gal. 6:11; 2 Thess. 3:17).

What is particularly striking about this set of farewell remarks is the mention of Artemas, Tychicus, Zenas, and Apollos. The personal names are an expression of the author's concern for succession in ministry. Artemas and Tychicus are to fill in for Titus, leaving him free to visit Paul. Zenas and Apollos are to be sent to their respective destinations by Titus. Paul effective delegates to Titus responsibility for sending other delegates on a mission. Thus, Zenas and Apollos are identified as second-generation delegates of the apostle. A plan for succession in ministry has been established.

- **12** Paul's ongoing pastoral care of communities that he had evangelized is reflected in his sending of delegates, particularly his trusted coworkers Timothy and Titus, to act in his stead when he himself was not able to visit. He sent Titus and a companion to Corinth (cf. 2 Cor. 7:13; 8:6, 18, 23; 12:18) and perhaps to Troas (2 Cor.

2:13). He sent Timothy to Corinth (1 Cor. 4:17; 16:10), Thessalonica (1 Thess. 3:2, 6), and probably to Philippi, a place to which Epaphroditus was sent presumably at some other time (Phil. 2:19-30). The deuteron-Pauline Epistle to the Colossians reflects this tradition of Paul's sending delegates on a mission to one or another place by mentioning that Paul sent Tychicus and Onesimus to Colossae (Col. 4:7-9).

Paul's pastoral concern for the churches is also reflected in the tradition that Paul had told Titus to remain in Crete (Titus 1:5) and Timothy to remain in Ephesus (1 Tim. 1:3). This tradition attests to the early church's desire for succession in the ministry of the gospel. Another expression of the early church's concern that a community not be without its ministers – and from the author's perspective not without a minister who was familiar with the apostle – is found in verse 12. Paul is described as eagerly desiring to have Titus come to him (Titus 3:12). He wants to have him at his side as soon as possible (cf. 2 Tim. 4:9, 11, 13, 21). To replace Titus on Crete, Paul is sending Artemas or Tychicus. When the replacement arrives, Titus can leave the island and go to meet Paul in the port city of Nicopolis.

The use of personal names in the epistle's final periscope lends a degree of verisimilitude to the entire text. Artemas, like so many other characters in the Pastorals, is not mentioned elsewhere in the New Testament. Tychicus is not mentioned in Paul's own letters but is presented as having been at Paul's side in five of the New Testament's post-Pauline books (cf. Acts 20:4; Eph. 6:21; Col. 4:7; 2 Tim. 4:12). Here Paul is presented as not having made a decision about which one of these two he should send. Either of them would be able to maintain the Pauline influence on the faith of the islanders during Titus' absence.

Nicopolis, *"city of victory,"* is the name of several imperial settlements that were established to commemorate a military victory. One of the cities named Nicopolis was built on the isthmus of the Bay of Actium, just across from the southern end of the Italian peninsula. The city was established to commemorate the naval victory of Augusts' forces over those of Mark Anthony in 31 B.C.E. Known as Nicopolos in Epirus (Tacitus, *Annals* 2.53) or Nicopolis of Achaia (Ptolemy, *Geography* 3.13), the city was a natural site for maritime transportation between Achaia and Italy. As the terminus of a trade route, it became an important commercial center and the site of quadrennial athletic games. Epictetus, the Stoic philosopher, arrived in the city as an exile in 89 C.E. (Gellius, *Attic Nights* 15.11.5).

This port city was a natural place for a person to pass the winter were he or she intending to take a sea voyage in the early spring when travel conditions became less treacherous than they would be in winter (cf. 1 Cor. 16:6; Acts 27:9-12). The Achaian port is probably the city that the author had in mind when he composed 3:12. A codicil to the epistle to Titus, first appearing in the 6th century Codex Coislinianus (H), says that the epistle *"was written by Paul the apostle to Titus, the first bishop of the Church of the Cretans upon whom hands had been laid, from Nicopolic of*

Macedonia." This note appears in most manuscripts of the Byzantine tradition. An 11th century minuscule (81) adds to the epistle an alternative form of the note: "*Written to Titus from Nicopolis in Crete.*" Two earlier manuscripts, the 5th century Codex Alexandrinus and the 9th century Codex Porphyrianus, append a simple notation, "*written from Nicopolis.*"

Paul often expressed a desire to visit those to whom he was writing. His letters were a substitute for his presence. Occasionally Paul gives a reason for why he was not immediately able to make the visit (cf. Rom. 15:22-29; 1 Cor. 16:5-9; 1 Thess. 2:18). His travelogues expand on his desire to visit those to whom he was writing and to provide substance for his expressed intention. In this epistle's travelogue, however, the fictive Paul expresses no desire to visit Crete or Titus. Rather, he asks that Titus make every effort to come to him (σπούδασον ἐλθεῖν). The real Paul, already deceased, remains absent from the community for who this text is really intended. Paul's protracted absence is a cover for the pseudepigraphic character of the epistle.

- **13 – 14** No more than Artemas does Zenas appear elsewhere in the New Testament. His name is a contraction of "*Ζηνοδοροσ,*" "*gift of Zeus.*" *Acts of Paul* 3.2 speaks of a man named Zeno as one of the sons of Onesiphoros. As the otherwise unknown Alexander is identified by his coppersmith's trade in 2 Tim. 4:14, so Zenas is identified by his profession. He is a lawyer, but the author does not indicate whether Zenas is versed in Greek, Roman, or Jewish law. According to the Greek menologies, Zenas was the first bishop of Diospolis of Lydda in Palestine. The tradition claims that he wrote a letter to Titus.

In contrast to Zenas, Apollos was a well-known figure in early Christianity. He is mentioned frequently in 1 Corinthians (1 Cor. 1:12; 3:4, 5, 6, 22; 4:6; 16:12), a sign that he was well known in the Achaian area. Acts 18:24-19:1 describes Apollos as an Alexandrian who was well versed in the Scriptures. He was catechized by Aquila and Priscilla and instructed in the ways of the Lord. Paul once tried to send Apollos back to visit the Corinthian community, but Apollos was reluctant to go (1 Cor. 16:12).

Titus is to get Zenas and Apollos prepared for their trip. The language recalls the language of the previous verse; Titus is to send delegates and he is to make every effort to come. The compound form of the verb in verse 13 connotes both *"send on one's way"* and *"prepare for a journey"* by providing money, food, companions, some means of travel, or whatever else is needed for a trip. In the light of the appended clause *"make sure that they lack nothing that they need,"* this second nuance must be incorporated into the meaning of the author's "πρόπεμψον" (cf. Rom. 15:24; 1 Cor. 16:6, 11; 2 Cor. 1:16). Hence the translation, *"Get Zenas ... and Apollos ready and send them on their way."*

In the narrow epistolary context of Titus, the next verse (v. 14) is addressed to Titus as a bit of advice that he should give to Zenas and Apollos as he is about to send them on their way. Christian missionaries should be ready for the hardships that they are bound to face; they must be ready to face these difficulties, choosing always to do good deeds no matter what the circumstances. *"Good deeds"* would be a secularized euphemism for the proclamation of the gospel in word and in work. In this narrow epistolary context, *"our people"* designates Zenas and Apollos.

In the broader context of this pseudepigraphic epistle, Zenas and Apollos belong to the author's narrative plot just as much as do *"Paul"* and *"Titus."* Zenas may have been a historical figure whose character has been lost because he is otherwise unknown to us. Both Zenas and the relatively well-known Apollos function in the narrative scene as exemplary figures. The paraenesis of verse 14 thus acquires broader significance. It is an exhortation not only for missionaries but for all of *"our people."* In fact, the expression *"choose good works"* is found in the author's final exhortation (Titus 3:8), where it clearly has a pragmatic, activity-oriented sense.

In the exhortation of 3:8, the good deeds are clearly that – namely, deeds that are beneficial for human beings. The author uses similar language in 3:14 to say that Titus should exhort Zenas and Apollos as he sends them out *"so that they are not ineffective."* The early church often used the imagery of growth and fruit in its kerygmatic discourse. This idiom evoked the positive effect of the proclamation of the gospel (cf. Matt. 13:8; Mark 4:7, 8; Luke 8:8). Matthew and Luke, appropriating Q material, write about *"fruit"* to describe a person's action (Matt. 3:8, 10; 7:16-20; 12:33; Luke 3:8-9; 6:43-44; 8:8).

Paul often expressed some concern about the effectiveness of his proclamation of the gospel. He feared that his efforts might prove to be *"empty"* or *"futile"* (1 Cor. 15:10, 14, 58; 2 Cor. 6:1; Gal. 2:2; Phil. 2:16; 1 Thess. 2:1; 3:5). Occasionally Paul used agricultural imagery to speak about his ministry (1 Cor. 3:5-9; 9:10-11), but he did not speak of its fruit, nor did he speak about its possible fruitlessness. The language of fruitlessness is the language that the author uses to express Paul's fears about the success of his preaching, his fears that his efforts would be in vain. This expression of concern is ironic; the very existence of post-Pauline texts such as the Letter to Titus shows that Paul's preaching had not been in vain.

- **15** Like most of Paul's letters, the Letter to Titus closes with various greetings. Paul often expressed third person greetings (Rom. 16:21-23; 1 Cor. 16:19-20a; 2 Cor. 13:12b; Phil. 4:21b-22; Phlm. 23-24). He even sent greetings on behalf of all his Christian siblings (1 Cor. 16:20a), all the churches (Rom. 16:16b), and all God's holy people (2 Cor. 13:12b; Phil. 4:22). Titus 3:15 says that *"everybody with me"* sends greetings. This unusual formula enhances the epistolary character of the author's text.

Paul often asked that his correspondents convey his best wishes to others. He included second person greetings in his letters to the Romans, Corinthians, Philippians, and Thessalonians (Rom. 16:3-16a; 1 Cor. 16:20b; 2 Cor. 13:12a; Phil. 4:21a; 1 Thess. 5:26). In verse 15 Titus is asked to convey greetings to *"those who love us in faith."* This unique combination of words underscores the formulaic nature of the expression *"in faith"* in the Pastoral Epistles (1 Timothy, 2 Timothy, and Titus).

Hellenistic letters customarily ended with a final greeting, sometimes in the author's own hand. The closing salutation of this letter, *"Grace be with all of you,"* is one of the shortest in the Pauline corpus (cf. 1 Tim. 6:21b; Col. 4:18). The finale of Paul's own letters always expanded on the idea of *"grace"* he always wrote *"the grace of our Lord (or the Lord) Jesus Christ."* Sometimes instead of a simple pronoun, *"you,"* Paul mentioned the spirit of those to whom he was writing (Gal. 6:18; Phil. 4:23; Phlm. 25).

The final greeting is a kind of blessing on the gathered assembly. The greeting is in the plural as are the final greetings of 1 and 2 Timothy (1 Tim. 6:21; 2 Tim. 4:22). The plural number of the greeting stands in contrast with the single individuals to whom the letter was presumably addressed, that is, either Titus or Timothy. The final greeting of Titus, unlike the final greetings of the epistles to Timothy, is reinforced by the addition of *"all"*: *"Grace be with all of you."*

The final section of the Letter to Titus looks to the future, that is, the missions of Artemis, Tychicus, Zenas, and Apollos, relatively unknown people who were continue the mission of the apostle. The pericope concludes with a comprehensive blessing. Those who read the Letter to Titus today are well aware that the mission of Paul has indeed been continued by untold numbers of anonymous Christians and that, as a result, the entire church has indeed been blessed. It is now the people who read The Letter to Titus to extend that "*grace*" to others in somewhere, and perhaps be someone's "*Artemis, Tychicus, Zenas, and Apollos.*"

Bibliography

Barrett, K. *The Pastoral Epistles*. New Clarendon Bible. Oxford: Clarendon, 1963.

Bassler, Joutte. *1 Timothy, 2 Timothy, Titus*. Nashville: Abingdon, 1996.

Boring, M. Eugene, Fred B. Craddock. *The People's New Testament Commentary*. Louisville,KY: Westminster John Knox Press, 2009.

Bruce, F.F. *Zondervan Bible Commentary: One-Volume Illustrated Edition*. Grand Rapids, MI: Zondervan, 2008.

Carson, D.A, R.T. France, J.A. Motyer, and G.J. Wenham. *New Bible Commentary: 21st century edition*. Nottingham, England: Inter-Varsity Press, 1994.

Charlesworth, J. *The Old Testament Pseudepigrapha, 2 Vols*. Garden City, NY: Doubleday, 1985.

Collins, Raymond F. *I and II Timothy and Titus: A Commentary*. New Testament Library. Lousville, KY: Westminster John Knox, 2002.

Danker, Frederick William. *A Greek-English Lexicon of the New Testament and other Early Christian*

Literature Thrid Edition (BDAG). Chicago, IL: The University of Chicago Press, 2000.

Dibelius, M., H. Conzelmann. *The Pastoral Epistles*. Hermeneia. Philadelphia: Fortress, 1972.

Dockery, David S. *Concise Bible Commentary*. Nashville, TN: B&H Publishing Group, 2010.

Douglas, J. D. *New Bible Dictionary 3rd ed*. Nottingham, England: Inter-Varsity Press, 1996.

Eum, Terry Kwanghyun. *Kata Markon*. North Charleston, SC: CreateSpace, 2015.

Eum, Terry Kwanghyun. *Pros Philemona*. North Charleston, SC: CreateSpace, 2015.

Eum, Terry Kwanghyun. *Iakwbou*. North Charleston, SC: CreateSpace, 2015.

Harrisville, Roy A. *The Concept of Newness in the New Testament*. Minneapolis: Augsburg, 1960.

Henry, Matthew. *Zondervan NIV Matthew Henry Commentary*. Grand Rapids, MI: Zondervan. 1992.

Mounce, William D. *Mounce's Complete Expository Dictionary of Old & New Testament Words*. Grand Rapids, MI: Zondervan. 2006.

Pendlebury, J.D.S. *The Archaeology of Crete*, 1939.

Wood, D. R. W. *New Bible Dictionary*. Nottingham, England: Inter-Varsity Press, 1996.

Index of Ancient and Biblical References

Index of Ancient and Biblical References

Index of Ancient and Biblical References

Index of Ancient and Biblical References

Index of Ancient and Biblical References

Index of Ancient and Biblical References

Made in the USA
Coppell, TX
24 September 2021

62887970R00066